YOUR FINANCIAL
UNIVERSE

THE A TO Z OF FINANCIAL LITERACY
FOR TEENAGERS AND YOUNG ADULTS

Jennifer Noonan

Jennifer Noonan

Published by Jennifer Noonan

First published in 2024 in Melbourne, Australia

Copyright © Jennifer Noonan

Website: www.yourfinancialuniverse.com.au

The moral rights of the author have been asserted.

Edited by Kate Victory Hannisian

ISBN (PBK) 978-0-646-70837-9

ISBN (ebook) 978-0-646-70838-6

Oak trees grow from acorns, but you gotta water them.

This book is dedicated to all of the young adults and teenagers who may not have received the education or resources that they needed to support their knowledge of all things financial. I hope this book helps you on your path to set up your financial future.

A special dedication to my family and special nephews and nieces who provided guidance and ideas along the way.

TABLE OF CONTENTS

PREFACE

When I was young, I remember getting up on a Sunday morning and heading out to our magazine delivery round. The day before, Dad would have picked up the magazine bundles from our neighbour and got them ready to deliver. As there were no rounds available close to where we lived at the time, my dad used to drive my three brothers and me about 25 minutes away to our delivery area. I remember it being very hilly and with grand old houses and big blocks.

It usually took us about two to three hours between us all and then we'd all hop back into the car and head home. I recall having black and coloured dye all over my hands from the magazines and papers. Dad would then 'pay' us for our delivery efforts. I can't recall exactly how much it was, but I think it was about $2! I used to love getting my $2 note and putting it away. **We did our work, and we received our reward. It was a direct and tangible link.**

I'm now a mum and wondering where that link is and how young people in particular are missing that link between work and reward. We now have bank accounts and don't see the money 'go in' as direct reward for our work. We do our shifts or referee our basketball game or deliver our papers and then magically two, three sometimes seven or fourteen days later it appears in our bank account. We have lost the direct link between our working effort and our reward. And we work hard. We miss gatherings and parties, have to get ourselves to work even if we are feeling under the weather or tired and have to manage our time between work, study, hobbies, sport and life in general. It's hard! So why don't we know more about our money? And how it can work for us? And how we can avoid losing it or spending it on things with no value?

Interestingly, in July 2020 and February-March 2021, the Australian Securities and Investments Commission (ASIC) conducted two surveys with young people aged 15 to 21 years. The intention of the survey was to understand how young Australians are positioned to learn about and engage with their finances, as well as how they feel about their finances and their financial well-being. Some of the key findings indicate a willingness to engage with the financial system and learn more about managing their finances, and that young peoples' experiences with money, as they grow and develop, shape how they feel and understand finances. However, a majority also reported that finding easy-to-use and relevant information is difficult and that there was little relevant education provided at school (*Young People and Money*, December 2021).

This book focuses on providing the RIGHT information and teaching teenagers and young adults about all things money from A to Z! And like the colour of our eyes and the size of our feet, to some degree our money habits are hereditary or part of our personality. We also learn from our parents and often mirror what they do, that being nurture. It's funny though, I have three children and despite seeing the same parents' financial behaviours, they all have quite different views on money, particularly on how they value money, and their saving versus spending preferences.

Financial literacy and understanding the basics of money, the economy, and our tax system are key life skills and can set you up for the life you are going to live. As a financial planner, over the years I have seen that the privilege of choice is the best position we can aim for, with financial pressures being a significant cause of household stress and anxiety. If you can learn the basics early, you are setting yourself up with positive financial habits and knowledge that will help you now and into the future, allowing you to be in control of your financial position. You work hard for your money, so understand the system within which you earn it, and how it can also work hard for you! As Malcom X once said, *'The future belongs to those who prepare for it today.'*

HOW TO USE THIS BOOK

This book is intended to provide a basic understanding of everything financial and provide you with the knowledge and tools to best manage your own financial situation. It isn't intended to be read from cover to cover, though you can if you like. It is set up in an A-to-Z format so that you can easily navigate to the topic that you are interested in or want to learn more about. Don't know how to get a tax file number? Navigate directly to T!

Throughout the book there are some case studies of my nephews and nieces, friends and family who have been where you may be now. These are designed to give you ideas of what other people in your situation or with similar goals to your own are doing and what they would like to do in the future. There is also one question that is common to each of the case studies, *"What's your definition of financial freedom?"* If you can answer that question, then you already have a goal, and this book can help you get there.

There are some symbols along the way to get you thinking about your own position and if necessary, take action.

ACTION: *Things you may want to look at, review and/or change for your own situation.*

KEY TIP: *Practical hints or tips about the topic that you can apply.*

RELATED TOPIC: *Other sections of the book that can add to your understanding.*

CASE STUDY: *Refer to the case study to read how someone else has learned about and/or used the topic in their life.*

At the end of the book, you can also create an individual action plan and set yourself some lifestyle and financial goals.

And a final word that relates to the ASIC survey on young people and money. 'The surveys revealed that sizeable proportions of young people are harbouring concerns about their financial situation, both now and into the future. In 2021, only half of young people agreed or strongly agreed with the statement "I am confident that I will be financially secure in adult life". Even fewer agreed or strongly agreed that "I am comfortable with my financial situation at the moment"' (Young People and Money – Survey Snapshot, December 2021, P. 13). It's a clear picture that young people are certainly facing challenges when it comes to their financial well-being.

So welcome to the world of all things financial! Expand your financial universe and set yourself up for success. Good luck!

A

AFTERPAY

Afterpay is the modern version of layby. It lets you buy today and pay later! One of the key differences between layby and Afterpay is that with Afterpay the consumer gets the goods straight away on payment of the first instalment before the entire amount is paid. With layby you had to visit the physical store and make a regular payment and couldn't pick up the purchase until full payment was made.

Afterpay allows you to buy something in four instalments over six weeks, with a 25% upfront payment amount. The outstanding amount doesn't incur any interest, however if you are unable to make a payment on time, a late payment fee is applied. The total late fees are capped at 25% of the order price, with a maximum payment of $68 per order.

> **KEY TIP:** *Make sure you have enough funds in your nominated account for each payment date. Diarise the payment due dates and set a reminder in your phone or on your calendar!*

Afterpay sets your spending limits, and they increase as your payment history is established. You can, however, set spending limits that you are comfortable with and can afford, which is a good way to monitor your spending.

Try to manage one order at a time. When you have multiple orders with multiple payment dates, not only can it add up to large regular payment obligations, but they become more difficult to manage and track (Afterpay: How It Works, 2024).

ALL ORDINARIES

You might hear people around you, or the media, refer to the 'All Ords'. This is referring to the oldest index of shares in Australia. It is a combination of each of the share prices for the largest 500 companies on the Australian

Stock Exchange. When the All Ordinaries is moving higher, it means that generally the Australian share market is performing well.

One thing to note is that the All Ordinaries is a market-weighted index, which is a method whereby the biggest companies in the market represent more of the index. This means that they have a bigger influence on the level on the index. When the All Ordinaries was introduced as an index, the starting base value was set at 500 on 31 December 1979 and trading started on 2 January. As at 1 January 2024, the index has been running 43 years and has grown to over 7,000 (History of the ASX - Market Index, 2024).

As the chart below indicates, the All Ords continues its upward trend despite numerous pullbacks, such as clearly shown in March 2020 when Covid-19 became a worldwide concern.

Source: Morgans Financial Limited, 2024

ASX

ASX stands for Australian Securities Exchange. This is the 'place' where shares are bought and sold. Shares need to be bought and sold through a *broker*. Brokers are people, organisations or platforms that execute your trades in the market.

There are really two key types of brokers: People or organisations who specialise in servicing share traders and investors such as Morgans Financial or Morgan Stanley; and online platforms that don't provide advice and usually have an online portal that displays your investments and allows you to simply trade online.

For each trade you will be charged *brokerage*, which is the fee for executing the trade on your behalf. The amount of brokerage will depend on whether you trade via a full-service broker (more expensive) or online (generally cheaper), and how often you trade.

The trading process looks something like this:

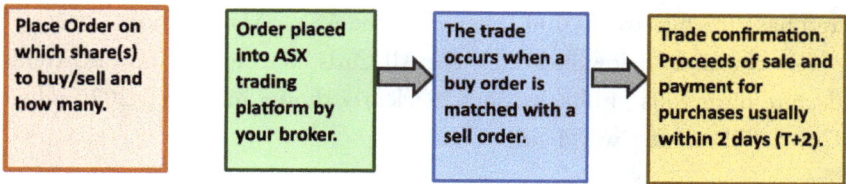

| Place Order on which share(s) to buy/sell and how many. | → | Order placed into ASX trading platform by your broker. | → | The trade occurs when a buy order is matched with a sell order. | → | Trade confirmation. Proceeds of sale and payment for purchases usually within 2 days (T+2). |

(ASX, Buying and Selling Shares and Investment Products on ASX, 2022)

Some of the lingo:

CHESS – When you buy your shares through a broker, your holdings are recorded in your name on the **CHESS subregister.** CHESS is the Clearing House Electronic Subregister System which is the computer system that the ASX uses to record shareholdings and manage share transactions. The first time you buy a share, you will receive a **Holder Identification Number (HIN)** which is like an account number. One HIN can be used for all of your investments listed on the ASX and is an important number for you to keep a record of and to keep safe. When you receive any dividend notices from your investment, usually your HIN number is listed on the top right-hand corner of the notice.

SRN – Sometimes you may also buy or register your shares or other investments directly with the company or organisation actually issuing the shares. These are referred to as **issuer-sponsored holdings** and you will be allocated a **Security-holder Reference Number (SRN)** for each of your investments. This is different from a HIN as you will be issued a new and different SRN for each different investment you hold with that company.

Market Order – When you buy a share at market, you request to buy the share as soon as possible at the best prevailing market price.

Limit Order – A request to buy a share at a specific price. When you set the price for your limit order, the share will only be automatically bought on your behalf when that price becomes available (Morningstar Investing Basics, 2018).

ASSET CLASSES

According to the Cambridge Dictionary, an asset is 'an item of property owned by a person or company, regarded as having value'. From an investment perspective, an asset is something that we can invest into, that has economic value to us.

There are four key asset classes: cash, fixed interest, property and shares.

Cash simply refers to having our money in the bank. Whether it is a regular or high-interest savings account, you earn interest based on your savings balance. Cash is very secure, and the capital amount of money that you invest won't go up and down in value.

Fixed Interest is when you invest a lump sum into an investment for a set period of time which earns interest along the way. At the end of the term, you get your lump sum back plus interest or you can reinvest the full amount (original plus interest) for another term. These types of investments are generally considered very safe.

Property is a very common investment in Australia. The type of property investment available ranges from the house we live in through to a commercial warehouse or a retail shopping centre! Property is considered a growth asset, as investors are seeking an increase in the capital value of the land or the property over time. Property might also produce income in the way of rent if the property has tenants.

Shares — Sometimes also referred to as equities, stocks or securities. These are investments in businesses that are listed on a stock exchange. When you purchase a share, you are buying a piece of that company. For example, if I buy 10 ANZ shares, I own a small piece of ANZ. I'm hoping that the price of my share goes up, which means it is increasing in capital value. Along the way the company may distribute their profits to you as a shareholder. This is income in the form of a **dividend**.

Cash and fixed interest are considered primarily income and conservative assets whereas property and shares are considered primarily growth assets. This is important in terms of the returns that are generated as well as the risk that is involved. It is expected that the higher the risk, the higher the potential return.

RELATED TOPICS
T – Term Deposit

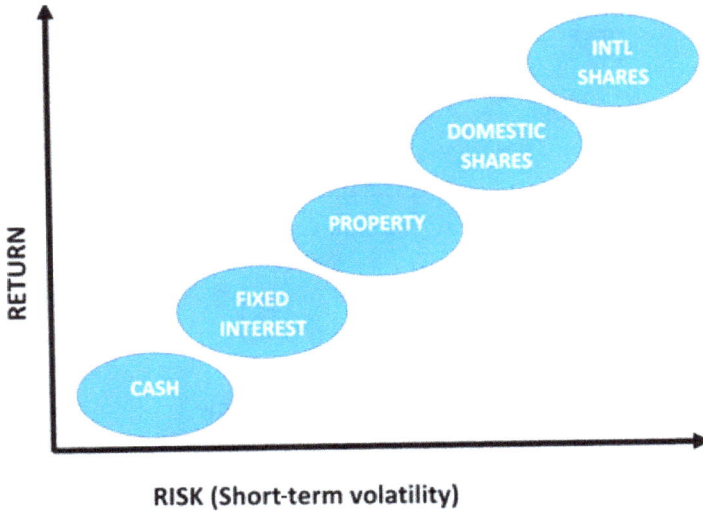

RISK (Short-term volatility)

Alternative assets – Some investment managers and superannuation funds also have a category labelled 'alternative assets'. These don't fit the traditional labels and include investments such as infrastructure, private equity, joint ventures, and commodities such as gold. This asset class is generally accepted as a higher-risk category focused more on high capital growth rather than income.

ASSET ALLOCATION

When we invest, we allocate our money into the different asset classes discussed above. The way that we allocate our funds will determine the overall return that we will receive and the overall risk of our portfolio. If we have a higher allocation to the more secure assets of cash and fixed interest, our portfolio will have less risk but will also achieve a more conservative or lower return. And the opposite is true too: the higher the allocation to assets such as property and shares, the higher the risk with an expected higher return.

Asset allocation should be aligned to the way we feel about investing, as well as what return we need to generate. Taking on a risky portfolio may be great when there is the opportunity for high return but it also means higher risk and that our investment will go up and down in value much more than a secure investment. We need to make sure that whatever asset allocation we choose, it meets our needs, and we can still sleep at night without worrying about our investments.

Asset allocations are often classed into various categories according to the 'mix' of investments. The percentage allocation will depend on the particular fund; some of the most common asset allocations include:

- $ **Income / Low Growth** – 75% income 25% growth
- $ **Balanced** – 50% income 50% growth
- $ **Growth** – 75% growth 25% income
- $ **High Growth** – 85% growth 15% income

The asset allocation pie chart below would be indicative of a more Balanced investor with up to 60% in growth and 40% in income-producing investments.

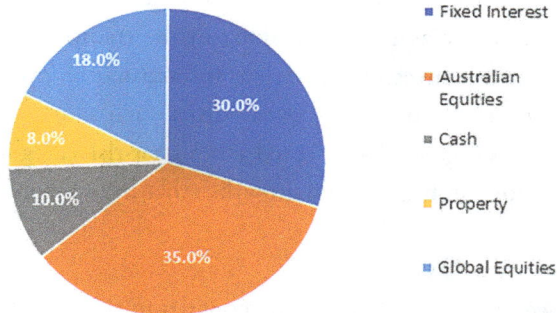

The other component to consider when you decide how you allocate your investment across the asset classes is **time**. If we need our money or a portion of our funds to be easily accessible, we should direct funds to assets that are easy to convert to cash. If we have a longer time horizon, we may be more willing to invest in higher-risk assets as we have time to ride out the ups and downs of that investment and are less in danger of having to liquidate (cash out) our investment at a time when the value is down.

The most important thing to remember about asset allocation is that it will determine the amount of portfolio risk your investment will be exposed to, as well as the expected returns it will generate.

ACTION: Review your asset allocation for your investments including superannuation. Prepare a pie chart if you can and consider whether it meets your needs.

Are you comfortable with your investment mix? If you want to change your investment exposure, you don't have to do it all at once and can make changes slowly over time. This could avoid large changes in the value of your investment all at one time.

B

BANKS

According to Britannica Money, a bank is 'an institution that deals in money and its substitutes and provides other money-related services. In its role as a financial intermediary a bank accepts deposits and makes loans' (Britannica Money, 2024). In Australia we have many banks that we can access, however it is estimated that the 'Big 4', including ANZ, Commonwealth, National Australia Bank and Westpac, have a combined market share of over 80% of banking, including deposits and lending (The AuFinance.com, 2024).

In Australia our banks are considered very stable and secure and are heavily regulated to ensure that they maintain financial viability and that when we go to the ATM to withdraw our money, we will be able to do so. In addition, the government has in place a **Financial Claims Scheme** that provides protection for deposit-holders with authorised deposit-taking institutions (ADIs – basically banks, building societies and credit unions). The government provides a safety net of up to $250,000 per account holder in the event that the ADI goes under! There is a list of every financial institution (or ADI) to which the scheme applies on the bank regulator's website (*APRA - Australian Prudential Regulation Authority, 2024*).

BASIC ACCOUNTING EQUATION

The basic accounting equation is:

Assets = Liabilities + Owner's Equity

Assets are something that 'provides a future economic benefit' (Accounting Triangle, Accounting Elements, 2024). Examples include land, building, and shares.

Liabilities are 'a future economic sacrifice you are obliged to make' (Accounting Triangle, Accounting Elements, 2024). This may be a debt owed or use of credit in purchasing an item.

Owner's Equity is defined as 'the residual interest in assets of the entity after deduction of its liabilities. This is the difference between assets and liabilities' (Accounting Triangle, Accounting Elements, 2024).

It is useful to understand this basic equation as it is used to indicate the profitability of the business. A healthy business has a balance between assets and liabilities, with good owners' equity.

Another basic equation that is useful is:

Gross Profit = Revenue less Expenses

Revenue represents money or income that is earned by the business. For example, revenue received for sales such as sales of TVs or services such as a haircut.

Expenses are the costs of running the business to produce income. For example, wages, taxes or raw materials.

Ideally businesses run at a profit so that they are earning more than they are spending.

BENEFICIARY

A beneficiary is the person you nominate to receive all or some of your assets on your death. This may be a nomination inside your superannuation fund, on a life insurance policy or in your will. It's important that you do nominate a beneficiary so that you can control and direct who receives your financial assets.

One of the areas that we all need to address is within our superannuation. If we do not nominate a beneficiary, the trustee of the superannuation fund decides where our money goes! There are three different types of nominations within superannuation:

- **Non-binding** – You nominate a beneficiary for the trustee to consider; however the trustee has full discretion.
- **Binding** – This type of nomination remains in force for three years from the date of signing and it must be followed by the trustee. There are specific requirements for binding nominations, such as it being witnessed by two

independent witnesses and each beneficiary must have a percentage allocated to them (i.e., 100%).

- **Non-lapsing Binding** – This nomination is essentially the same as a binding nomination; however it does not lapse until it is either revoked or changed. These provide certainty but need to be reviewed regularly, particularly when your circumstances change, such as marriage or divorce.

ACTION: Visit the website of your superannuation provider and log onto the member section or review your last statement to check your current beneficiary nomination. Remember, this is your hard-earned money so you should understand where it goes!

BOND

There are different types of bonds. We will look at two different types.

Investment Bond – A fixed interest investment. Bonds are issued by governments or companies. The investor contributes an investment amount (the principal), and the issuer pays a regular, fixed interest amount for the term of the investment. There are different terms available, ranging from one month through to a 10-year government bond.

At the end of the investment period (maturity), the amount you initially invested is repaid to you. These types of investments are effective for generating a steady income stream.

There are many different types of investment bonds, including government bonds, insurance bonds, company bonds (often used to raise capital for company projects for example), and funeral bonds.

Rental Bond – This is a deposit that is paid by a tenant to the landlord prior to the commencement of a lease. This is provided as security for any damage that may be done to the property or if there is still rent owing when you move out. The amount of the bond is different depending on the state or territory; however it is usually a minimum of four weeks' rent. At the end of the lease, you can apply for the bond to be released.

REAL LIFE FINANCIAL UNIVERSES
- The rental bond is an important cost to consider when you first move out and start life as a tenant. *Have a read of Alice's financial thoughts and the costs of moving out.*

BROKERS

You can think of a broker as a go-between. They represent you to another party and negotiate and arrange the contract. Usually, they will receive a commission or fee for their services. It is important to note that often the provider or lender funds the commission, so it doesn't come out of your pocket! There are several different types of brokers. A couple of brokers that can be very useful are:

$ *Mortgage broker* – assists borrowers connect with lenders and researches and negotiates the best and most suitable mortgage for the borrower. Mortgage brokers usually have access to many different lenders so that they can find the most appropriate loan. They can be used for your first loan or a refinance. Mortgage brokers also provide and assist with the paperwork along the way, which can be cumbersome, to put the loan in place.

$ ***Insurance broker*** – connects clients with insurance companies to find the most appropriate insurance solution, considering both cost and features and benefits. Similarly to mortgage brokers, they are not tied to one specific insurance company and can research many different insurance providers to find the best insurance product. They will also assist with the insurance application which can be lengthy and detailed. There are also online insurance brokers such as Compare the Market (ComparetheMarket.com.au).

BUDGET

A budget is a tool that allows you to track where you spend your money and identify whether you have a cash flow surplus or shortfall. The key elements of a budget include:

INS	OUTS
Salary	Mortgage / Rent
Investment Income	Insurances
Pensions	Utilities and Rates
Centrelink Payments	Entertainment and Subscriptions
	Transport / Vehicle Costs
	Healthcare
	Phone
	Groceries / Food
	Childcare / Schooling

The inputs to everyone's budget will be different and will often depend on what life stage you are at. Try not to view a budget as a restriction but rather a tool that gives you choice. If you can identify where your money is going, you can make choices around where to spend it! If you set yourself some goals, you can use your budget to achieve them. **Refer to the Goals Template in the Appendix.**

There are many different budgeting apps that you can have on your phone, or you can simply use an Excel spreadsheet to add everything up for you! One of my favourite money sites for education and information is the Moneysmart website that has been developed by the Australian Securities and Investment Commission (ASIC). There is a basic budgeting tool that you could use as a start. The website is: Budget planner - Moneysmart.gov.au

Budgeting Tips

- Pay the necessities first. Remember needs versus wants!
- Set up monthly bills for utilities so that you are not hit by big bills all at once. This evens out your cash flow.
- Focus on using any surplus to repay debt, particularly high-interest credit cards.
- Track your spending and set some goals for your money. Setting goals gives you 'money mindfulness' and awareness of where your money is being spent. If you don't like what you see, you can change it!
- Consider having separate accounts that meet your different needs – one for everyday bills, one for spending and one for saving. Ideally your savings account is more difficult to access so the temptation to use it is less.

Are You a Spender or a Saver?

Usually, most people tend to be either a spender or a saver! Neither is right or wrong; however, being aware of your preference can give insight into your behaviour. There's no point saving all your money in a bank account and not experiencing all that life has to offer. But there's also no point in ongoing spending where you end up in financial stress and unable to make ends meet. There are lots of different quizzes on the internet that will give you some insight into where you sit.

Striking a Balance

Whichever side you lean toward, remember something: It's important to find balance between the two. If you focus solely on spending, you could end up with lots of debt. If the only thing you do is save, you don't get to enjoy the things money can provide you, such as giving, going on a nice holiday, or having the occasional night out.

REAL LIFE FINANCIAL UNIVERSES
- Have a read of Jack and Sophie's approach to budgeting and saving to help save for a house deposit, or Angus trying to budget his part time earnings.

C

CAPITAL

Capital refers to the initial lump sum amount of your investment. When your capital is invested in growth assets, you are seeking capital growth so that the value of your investment increases. When you sell your investment at an increased value, it is referred to as a capital gain.

And vice versa when your capital investment doesn't do so well, and the value of your initial capital decreases. If you sell the investment at that time, it is referred to as a capital loss.

It is important to remember, particularly with capital losses, that the loss is **only realised** when you sell the asset. Ideally you can hold on to the asset until it gets into the capital growth zone again.

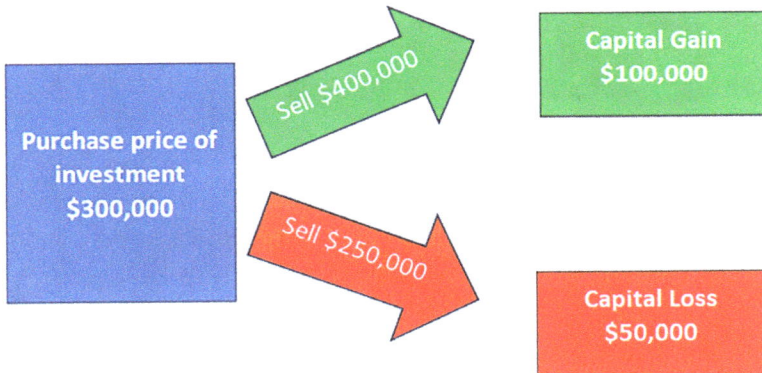

Purchase price of investment $300,000

Sell $400,000 → Capital Gain $100,000

Sell $250,000 → Capital Loss $50,000

CASH / MONEY

Cash is the physical form of currency or coins that can be exchanged to buy goods and services.

CASH FLOW

The way we manage our cash flow has a big impact on our ability to save and meet our goals. There is an old saying that *'Cash flow is king'*!

Getting on top of your cash flow starts with your budget, managing the cash that is coming in, understanding your expenses, and setting yourself some goals.

One of the most important things about managing cash flow is **to prioritise your 'needs' over your wants and repaying debt first**, particularly high-interest debt such as credit cards. Any surplus cash flow can then be allocated to your other necessary expenses such as utility bills, and finally your surplus cash flow can be directed to savings or investments.

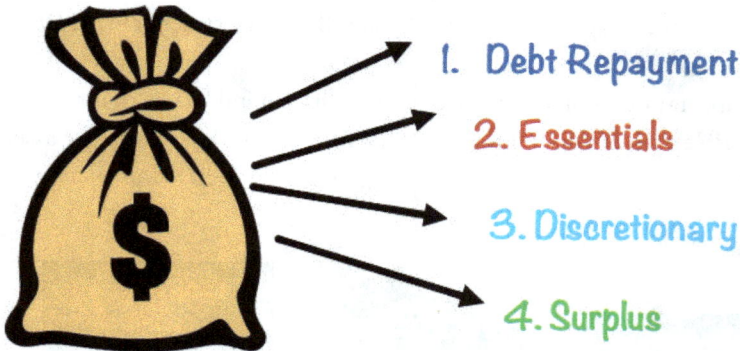

1. Debt Repayment
2. Essentials
3. Discretionary
4. Surplus

Using a form of prioritising where you direct your money helps keep you on top of debt and providing for your essentials. When you first start working, you may not have much left over in the surplus bucket, but even small amounts all add up. **Use the Goals Template in the Appendix to help set some cash flow goals.**

CENTRELINK

Centrelink is an Australian government body managed by Service Australia. It delivers social security payments and services to a range of different people with different needs including, families, unemployed, retirees, carers, people with disabilities, Indigenous people and students.

Some of the more common payments to students and young adults include:

Job Seeker – Assistance if you are older than 22 years of age and you are looking for work. It may also apply when you are sick or injured and unable to do your normal work or study for a short period of time.

Youth Allowance – Provides support to students and apprentices who are age 18 to 24 and studying or completing an Australian Apprenticeship full time.

Austudy – Is similar to the youth allowance, but it is for people over the age of 25.

Some Centrelink payments may also qualify for **Rent Assistance**, which is an additional payment to help with the cost of rent.

Most payments will have eligibility criteria such as an income and/or assets test. To check what payments are available and the different requirements, jump online to Centrelink - Services Australia.

COMPOUNDING

Compounding is a very simple but powerful wealth accumulation concept and a way of increasing the return on your investment. It is 'a method of calculating total interest on the principal where the interest earned is reinvested. For investors, it results in exponential growth of assets or capital' (Wall Street Mojo, 2024). The longer the interest is reinvested, the more quickly it grows. Importantly, you are not withdrawing any income or interest, but you are instead putting it straight back into the investment balance.

The example below highlights how we can use the simple process of compounding to our investment advantage.

Emma is **21 years old** and has started her first job.

She decides to save **$2,600 a year ($50 per week)** until she is 30.

Her investment earns **7% per annum.**

When she turns 30, she doesn't make any further contributions, but she continues to maintain her investment.

Her friend Timothy waits until he is **31.**

He then starts saving **$2,600 per annum ($50 per week).** He continues to contribute his **$2,600** per annum from **age 31 until he is 65.**

His investment also earns **7% per annum.**

Emma contributes $26,000 over 10 years, whereas **Timothy contributes $91,000** over **35 years** until retirement at age 65. However, at age 65 Emma has a balance of $410,380 whilst Timothy has a balance of $384,575.

You can see the vast difference in earning that resulted from Emma starting early and then leaving the investment to grow and compound. Emma has contributed $65,000 LESS than Timothy and ended up with $25,805 MORE at age 65.

It's great that Timothy started later; however he is always behind due to the power of early compounding that Emma achieves.

It's important to see that you don't have to save a large amount to achieve the effect of compounding. If you start early, you have time working on your side.

Superannuation savings take advantage of compounding in that we put away regular amounts via our employer and personal superannuation contributions and are unable to access our money in most cases until we reach retirement.

> **KEY TIP:** *Investing early gives you a great start. There are other important considerations when you start out, many of which are covered in this book, such as diversification and risk. The Moneysmart website also has a useful investor toolkit that can help you get started.*
>
> Investor toolkit - Moneysmart.gov.au

CREDIT

Credit has several meanings. One definition, according to the Collins Dictionary, is that 'If you are allowed **credit**, you are allowed to pay for goods or services several weeks or months after you have received them' (Collins English Dictionary, 2024). This is essentially how Afterpay works! **Credit** can also refer to your bank account. If your bank account is in credit, that means you have money in the account.

Lastly, we may refer to **credit** in association with money that we borrow from a bank or financial institution that we have access to spend and we pay interest on that amount. Often banks set up a line of credit so that you can have access to funds as you need them and you are only charged interest on the amount you have spent, not the full amount of credit that you have been given.

CREDIT CARDS

A credit card is a card issued by a money provider (such as a bank), that allows you to spend their money rather than your own for everyday purchases. There is usually a period such as 30 days during which if you repay the amount owing in full, you will not be charged interest. However, when you don't repay the monthly amount owed in full you will be charged interest on the balance which is usually significantly higher than other forms of credit, and often up to around 18%.

Your card will have a *credit limit* which is the maximum amount you can spend on your card. Whilst credit cards can be used effectively to purchase goods and services and you often receive benefits for the amount spent, such as Qantas points, you should aim to repay the balance every month.

Credit card debt is usually considered 'bad' debt as the money is used for goods and services that are disposable or depreciating assets (such as TVs or household goods) and you pay a higher level of interest. Use credit cards wisely and try to keep spending low.

CREDIT CARD TIPS:

Keep your credit limit low and manageable.

- *Try to only have one credit card.*
- *Repay the full balance monthly.*
- *If you can't pay in full, prioritise repaying this debt as it has a higher interest rate that will accrue.*

CREDIT SCORE

Your credit score is a 'score' given to you that reflects your personal and financial information and any previous loans/credit that you have taken out. Your credit score is maintained by various credit reporting agencies and depends on the level of your previous lending, how many applications you have made and your repayment history such as whether you pay on time. It generally ranges from zero to 1,000 and the higher the score, the better your credit rating.

Your credit rating is used by lender to assess your eligibility for loans, the interest rate you may get and the amount of debt that they will provide you. You can access your credit score from many different sources. Visit

CreditSmart to understand what your score means and where to obtain it. Credit Report Check - Get My Credit Score Free - CreditSmart.

CREDIT UNIONS

Credit unions are like banks and offer financial products such as savings accounts, credit cards and loans; however, they are non-profit organisations. Whilst banks share their profits with shareholders, credit unions put any profit back into their organisation and products. Because of this they may offer lower and more competitive rates, providing an alternative to the big banks.

Credit unions were once membership based and often related to an area or occupation such as the Police Credit Union. There are now about 40 credit unions available to the public in Australia, the largest being Credit Union Australia (theaufinance.com, 2024).

CURRENCY

Currency is simply the money used to buy goods and services in a particular country. For example, the Australian dollar, the Japanese yen or the European euro.

CYBERSECURITY

According to IBM, cybersecurity is 'the practice of protecting critical systems and sensitive information from digital attacks' (IBM, 2024).

We all have a lot of day-to-day interactions and transactions online, whether it is transferring money from one bank account to another or interacting with friends via Facebook or Instagram. Cybercrime in general, including online scams and SMS or email phishing, is a growing concern and there have been multiple high-profile cases where information has been accessed and sold by hackers, often via the dark web. It is important that we are vigilant about ensuring the security of our information and any systems that we use, to prevent our personal and sensitive information being illegally accessed by others.

ScamWatch Australia alone reports that almost **$570 million** was lost in scams in 2022 (ScamWatch, 2024)!

The Australian Cyber Security Centre is a government organisation that promotes cyber safety and provides warnings and support for cyber security threats. It also provides the general public with information on how to protect yourself online (The Australian Signals Directorate, cyber.gov.au, 2024).

D

DEBT

Put simply, debt is an amount of money that you owe someone, whether that is your parents, your bank, or the government.

Good versus Bad Debt

We can divide debt into good debt and bad debt – it depends on what you are using the debt for. If you are borrowing to buy an asset that will **grow** such as a mortgage on a house or borrowing to buy shares, this is **good** debt as the value of those assets will grow over time.

In contrast, if we use debt to buy assets such as cars for example, that is considered 'bad' debt. The minute you drive that car out of the car dealer it loses value (see Depreciation below). You are paying interest on an asset that is going down in value.

> *Let's say I borrow money to purchase a brand-new Kia Cerato at a cost of $30,000. I pay regular interest on my loan and get use of the new car. As the car ages the value depreciates and after three years it is now worth around $22,000. I am still paying interest but as soon as I drive my new car out of the showroom, it loses value.*
>
> *Alternatively, I borrow $30,000 to buy ANZ shares. Over the last three years the value of these shares has grown by around 25% as well as providing dividends of around 5%. This means that my interest payments are covered by the growth in the value of my investment.*
>
> *No investment is guaranteed to grow in value but 99% of all new cars are going to depreciate in value.* ☹

The other thing you need to consider with your debt is the relationship between the amount of debt and the value of the asset. For example if I own my home valued at $1 million and have a mortgage of $500,000, the **loan-to-valuation ratio** is 50%. That is, I own 50% of my home.

It is important to understand this ratio when you are borrowing, as lenders will use this as a guide to how much they will allow you to borrow. Usually, lenders will allow you to borrow up to 90% but you may have to pay either a higher interest rate or take out mortgage lenders insurance if it is related to a home mortgage. The lower the loan-to-valuation ratio, the better it is!

KEY DEBT TIPS:

- *Use debt to grow your wealth, not depreciate it!*
- *Understand and monitor your loan-to-valuation ratio (LVR).*

DEFICIT

A deficit means that there is an excess of spending or liabilities over income or assets. A common use of the term deficit is in relation to the government budget. When the budget is in deficit it means that government spending is greater than government revenue (such as taxes). When it is in surplus, the government is bringing in more revenue than it is spending.

DEPRECIATION

Depreciation is the reduction in value of an asset over time due to wear and tear. In accounting terms it is a 'method used to allocate the cost of a tangible or physical asset over its useful life. Depreciation represents how much of an asset's value has been used' (What Is Depreciation, and How Is It Calculated? Investopedia.com, 2024).

It is important to note that depreciation is considered a **COST!** So going back to our notion of good versus bad debt, it reinforces not using debt to accumulate assets that are depreciating. You are paying interest in addition to the cost of the asset losing value! *A double whammy!*

DOLLAR-COST AVERAGING

Dollar-cost averaging is an investment strategy where the same **dollar value** of units is purchased across time, regardless of the value. This takes advantage of rising and falling markets and helps you buy **more** when the price is **low** and *less* when the price is *high*, **averaging out** the price you pay over time.

Let's look at an example where you consistently purchase $100 worth of units at intervals, as the price per unit rises and falls:

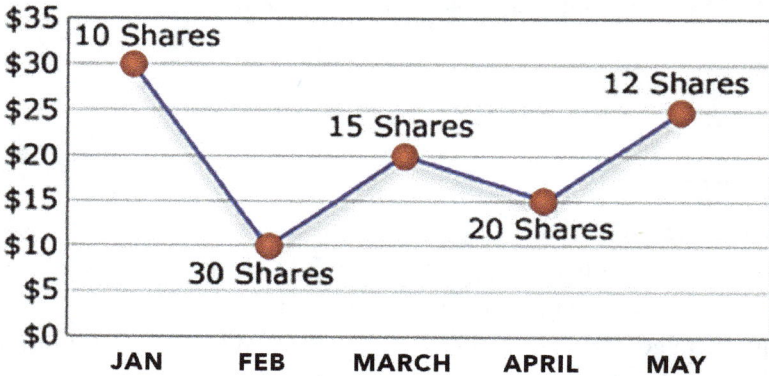

MONTH	INVESTMENT AMOUNT	UNIT PRICE	NUMBER OF UNITS PURCHASED
Jan	$300	$30	10
Feb	$300	$10	30
March	$300	$20	15
April	$300	$15	20
May	$300	$25	12
TOTAL	$1,500		87
		AVERAGE COST PRICE $18.24	

Another benefit of dollar-cost averaging is the regular and ongoing dollar contribution into the investment. This can be set up for any investment in your own name, and we are forced to take this strategy within our superannuation. Each payday, our employer contributes to our superannuation and the superannuation fund buys units of our selected investment option, regardless of what the market prices are for the investments.

A dollar-cost averaging strategy means you are consistently investing without the stress of trying to time the market. If we could pick the highs and lows of the market reliably over time then we would all be multimillionaires, but the fact is that most people can't do this!

KEY TIP:

- *Set up your investment with a regular contribution whether that is weekly, fortnightly or monthly. This way you are automatically dollar-cost averaging and not worrying about the price.*

DIVERSIFICATION

Diversification is fundamentally not 'putting all of your eggs in one basket'. This means that you have a little bit of your money invested in lots of different things.

Let's look at an example. If I had a $10,000 investment to diversify, I could spread my money across the different asset classes such as $2,000 in cash, $3,000 in property, $4,000 in Australian shares and $1,000 in international shares. Markets tend to move in different directions and so by having some of your money in different asset classes, not all of your money is affected.

We can see in the following table how different investments clearly go up and down at different times:

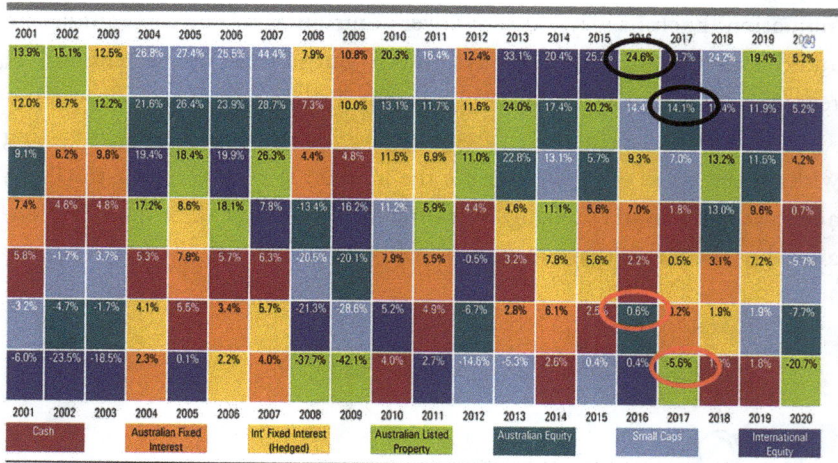

2001	2002	2003	2004	2005	2006	2007	2008	2009	2010	2011	2012	2013	2014	2015	2016	2017	2018	2019	2020
13.9%	15.1%	12.5%	26.8%	27.4%	25.5%	44.4%	7.9%	10.8%	20.3%	16.4%	12.4%	33.1%	20.4%	25.2%	24.6%	17%	24.2%	19.4%	5.2%
12.0%	8.7%	12.2%	21.6%	26.4%	23.9%	28.7%	7.3%	10.0%	13.1%	11.7%	11.6%	24.0%	17.4%	20.2%	14.4%	14.1%	14%	11.9%	5.2%
9.1%	6.2%	9.8%	19.4%	18.4%	19.9%	26.3%	4.4%	4.8%	11.5%	6.9%	11.0%	22.8%	13.1%	5.7%	9.3%	7.0%	13.2%	11.5%	4.2%
7.4%	4.6%	4.8%	17.2%	8.6%	18.1%	7.8%	-13.4%	-16.2%	11.2%	5.9%	4.4%	4.6%	11.1%	5.6%	7.0%	1.8%	13.0%	9.6%	0.7%
5.8%	-1.2%	3.7%	5.3%	7.8%	5.7%	6.3%	-20.5%	-20.1%	7.9%	5.5%	-0.5%	3.2%	7.8%	5.6%	2.2%	0.5%	3.1%	7.2%	-5.7%
-3.2%	-4.7%	-1.7%	4.1%	5.5%	3.4%	5.7%	-21.3%	-28.6%	5.2%	4.9%	-6.7%	2.8%	6.1%	2.5%	0.6%	1.2%	1.9%	1.9%	-7.7%
-6.0%	-23.5%	-18.5%	2.3%	0.1%	2.2%	4.0%	-37.7%	-42.1%	4.0%	2.7%	-14.6%	-5.3%	2.6%	0.4%	0.4%	-5.6%	1%	1.8%	-20.7%
2001	2002	2003	2004	2005	2006	2007	2008	2009	2010	2011	2012	2013	2014	2015	2016	2017	2018	2019	2020

Cash	Australian Fixed Interest	Int' Fixed Interest (Hedged)	Australian Listed Property	Australian Equity	Small Caps	International Equity

Source: Morningstar, Top Performing Asset Classes for 2019/20 (morningstar.com.au), 2020

Looking at the table above, let's say in **2016** all of my money is invested in Australian listed property. Given the 24.6% return, I'm jumping for joy! But if we just wait just one year and look at **2017**, then the opposite is true!

If we had instead invested in half Australian shares and half Australian listed property, the result would be much different, and the market extremes would have much less impact on our overall portfolio.

Often investments are automatically invested in a diversified manner. Take a look at your superannuation, for example. It is most likely invested in a diversified option such as a Conservative or Growth portfolio, which will invested in a bit of everything. Here's an example of the Balanced option in Australian Super:

Strategic asset allocation

ASSET CLASS	RANGE	ALLOCATION
Australian shares	10-45%	23.5%
International shares	10-45%	28.5%
Private equity	0-15%	4%
Unlisted infrastructure	0-30%	9%
Listed infrastructure	0-10%	1%
Unlisted property	0-30%	8%
Listed property	0-10%	1.5%
Credit	0-20%	4.5%
Fixed interest	0-25%	14%
Cash	0-20%	6%
Other assets	0-5%	0%

Source: AustralianSuper, Hands-Off & Diversified Super Account | AustralianSuper, 2024

DIVIDENDS

Dividends are payments made to shareholders out of the profits of the company. They can be cash payments made directly to the investor or they can be reinvested back into the company in the form of additional shares. Dividend payments are generally determined by the company's board of directors and are paid at a scheduled frequency, such as quarterly, half-yearly or annually.

Dividends can be *franked*, which means that the company has already paid tax on the dividend and the shareholder receives a franking credit. At tax time, the franking credit offsets the income from the dividend. For example, if I receive a *franked dividend* of $100 and the company has paid 30% tax on the income, then I will receive a $30 franking credit to apply to my dividend income. This means that I really only pay tax on $70, not the full $100.

RELATED TOPICS
S – Shares

If a dividend is *unfranked*, this means that all the income is taxable to the individual shareholder.

Not all shares pay a dividend; it depends on the company you have invested in. Some companies are focused on growth and achieving a higher share price, rather than paying out dividend income.

If you are interested in the dates that dividends are paid, you can check on the company's website or a general website such as Market Index.

https://www.marketindex.com.au/upcoming-dividends

E

EARNINGS

Earnings can be considered in several different contexts.

For an **individual** it may refer to the salary we earn from our jobs. An interesting statistic is average earnings for individuals in Australia, which you can look up at the Australian Bureau of Statistics website here: Average Weekly Earnings, Australia, May 2023 | Australian Bureau of Statistics (abs.gov.au)

For a **company,** earnings are the profits produced each term, which may be assessed quarterly or annually. If you are an investor in a company, you can watch and follow the company's earnings as they are generally considered to be a direct link to how well the company is performing. If the company is a listed company (on the ASX, for example) the earnings are released to the public. You can check all company information and announcements, including earnings, by accessing the ASX listing of companies (Company Directory, asx.com.au).

ECONOMY

According to the Oxford Dictionary, the economy is 'the relationship between production, trade and the supply of money in a particular country or region' (Oxford Learner's Dictionary, Oxford University Press, 2024).

The key elements of an economy can be seen in the diagram below.

THE ECONOMY

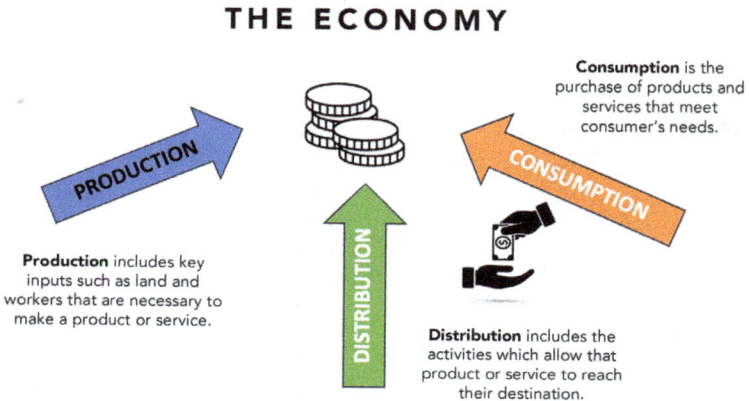

Consumption is the purchase of products and services that meet consumer's needs.

PRODUCTION

CONSUMPTION

DISTRIBUTION

Production includes key inputs such as land and workers that are necessary to make a product or service.

Distribution includes the activities which allow that product or service to reach their destination.

Source: Social Science, Elements in the Economy, 2019

Economics is the study of the economy and how it works. *Microeconomics* studies the individual elements including businesses and individuals and how they make decisions that affect the overall economy. *Macroeconomics*, on the other hand, looks at the big picture. It studies the impact of economy-wide indicators such as inflation and unemployment and how they affect the growth and success of the economy.

EQUITY

Equity has a few meanings, ranging from achieving equal outcomes, to the value of shares that a company issues. The key meaning and purpose of equity that we want to discuss here is in relation to any borrowings on assets.

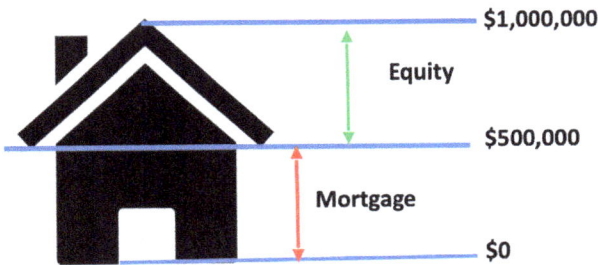

Equity in this sense means the value of property once the charges or borrowings have been deducted.

For example, let's say my house is worth $1,000,000 and I have a mortgage of $500,000. The equity I have in my house is $500,000 or 50% of the value of the property.

Equity is important as it is used by lenders in the assessment of how much they will allow you to borrow, and whether you require Lenders Mortgage Insurance (LMI). Most banks will require LMI if you want to borrow more than 80% of the value of the property, which means you have less than 20% equity in the property.

Most people increase the equity in their home by repaying their home mortgage and decreasing their loan balance. Equity is also increased by market forces. If your home increases in value, it affects

RELATED TOPICS

L – Loans

your equity. In our example above, if the value of the property increases to $1,500,000 and our loan remains at $500,000, the amount of equity we now own is $1,000,000 or 66.6% of the value of the property.

The other important note about equity is that we can use our existing equity to support additional borrowing for goals such as renovations, a deposit for an investment property, investing in shares or buying a new car. The amount of equity is factored into the bank's calculation of how much they will allow you to borrow as well as the traditional considerations such as income and living expenses.

ESTATE PLANNING

Estate planning, in simple terms, is the payment of the right amount, to the right people at the right time. Estate planning has many elements and whilst having a valid **will** is at the core of any estate plan, there are other considerations such as **powers of attorney** and making sure you have a binding death benefit nomination for your superannuation.

Estate planning is for everyone. It doesn't matter who you are or what you do, it is an essential considera-

RELATED TOPICS
B – Beneficiary
P – Power of Attorney

tion and the consequences of lack of planning can be significant. You want your hard-earned money to go to the people you want. There are many resources online that may be helpful, such as DIY will kits which may be suitable for simple situations.

Choice have done a good analysis of DIY will kits and reviewed some of the options available. Check out the website here: DIY will kits – how to draft your own will | CHOICE

ACTION: *Do you have a will in place?*
Have you considered who you would like to
receive your assets?

ETF – EXCHANGE TRADED FUND

An exchange traded fund (ETF) is a managed fund that you can buy or sell on the stock exchange (ASX) and trade like a share. An ETF is most often a passive investment in that the manager aims to track a particular index such as the ASX200 rather than actively manage the fund. ETFs are low cost as the aim of an ETF is to earn a return in line with the specified index it is tracking rather than outperform it. They are also an easy and effective way to diversify as they have exposure to multiple shares in one holding!

ETFs are available for a range of different asset classes such as Australian shares, property, global shares, as well as different commodities such as gold. When you invest in an ETF, you purchase units in the ETF and the ETF manager invests the funds and owns the underlying shares or assets.

EXCHANGE RATE

The exchange rate is the rate at which money of different countries can be exchanged for another. It also governs the terms for international trade and investment.

The most common reason for people to refer to the exchange rate is when they are planning a trip overseas and want to understand how much money one Australian dollar is valued in the foreign currency. For example, on average $1 AU will buy about 69 US cents.

F

FISCAL POLICY

Fiscal policy is enacted by the government to influence the economy by making changes to government spending and taxes. If the government wants to 'slow down' the economy, it can increase taxes and/or lower government spending (known as a fiscal contraction). This has the effect of reducing disposable income for consumers (as more of our salary is going to taxes) and lowering demand, which in turn lowers output.

On the flip side, if the government wants to stimulate the economy, it will increase spending and lower taxes (known as a fiscal expansion). Consumers have more money in their pockets and will stir demand with increased spending, which will lead to higher output. During the Covid-19 period for example, the government increased its spending significantly through measures such as the JobKeeper program to keep the economy active (Investopedia, Fiscal Policy: Balancing between tax rates and public spending, 2023).

G

GDP

GDP stands for gross domestic product (GDP). This is the market value of all final goods and services produced within a country over a specific period of time. GDP measures how well the economy produces the goods and services that people use, including necessities, conveniences, and luxuries. GDP is often discussed in the media as a key element that indicates the state of the economy.

One of the most used formulas for GDP is the <u>expenditure approach:</u>

GDP = C+G+I+NX

where:

C = Consumer Spending
G = Government spending
I = Investment
NX = Net exports (i.e., exports minus imports)

In Australia, the Australian Bureau of Statistics (ABS) collects data from households, companies and government agencies and uses three different calculations for GDP. The three definitions of GDP are:

- GDP (P): total value added from goods and services produced;
- GDP (I): total income generated by employees and businesses (plus taxes less subsidies); and
- GDP (E): total value of expenditure by consumers, businesses and governments on final goods and services' (RBA, Economic Growth, 2024).

The Reserve Bank of Australia (RBA) will then generally take the average of the three GDP indicators as shown in the diagram.

How is GDP Measured?

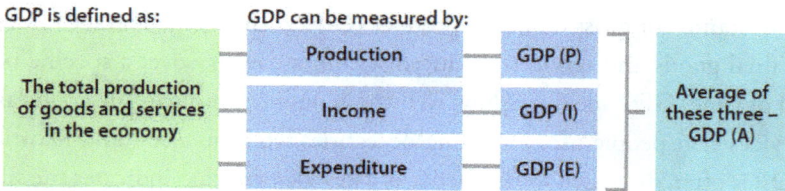

GDP is defined as:	GDP can be measured by:		
The total production of goods and services in the economy	Production	GDP (P)	Average of these three – GDP (A)
	Income	GDP (I)	
	Expenditure	GDP (E)	

The GDP growth rate then compares the year-on-year change of the measure to determine the growth of the economy over that period. GDP has a direct correlation to other measures such as unemployment, and so is a good measure of the health of an economy.

GEARING

Gearing is the strategy of borrowing money to invest. Gearing enables you to boost your investment earning power by increasing the amount of money you have available to invest. You can use your borrowed funds to purchase different assets and investments. Whilst gearing offers a 'boost' to your available funds, it is not for everyone and there are risks involved that you need to consider.

Generally, to be effective, a geared investment should:

- Generate a reliable long-term income flow which grows over the investment time frame. Ideally the income meets the interest repayment
- Be used for growth investments that grow in value over time (generate a capital gain).
- Be considered for investment time frames of five years or more.

BENEFITS	RISKS
Magnifies your returns if your investment increases in value	Magnifies your losses if your investment decreases in value. If your investments perform poorly, you may be left paying off a loan that is larger than the value of your investments
Increases the amount you can invest so you earn investment returns on a larger amount	If interest rates go up, you may not be able to meet your interest repayments
Potential tax advantages – the costs of borrowing are generally tax deductible	You may incur penalties or fees if you repay the loan sooner than agreed
You can achieve higher returns (after costs) than you could without borrowing	Net returns must be higher than your net interest costs for this strategy to be beneficial

A gearing strategy is not a quick fix and should be implemented over a long-term time frame as this allows enough time for you to benefit from the returns of growth assets and to ride out any short-term market fluctuations. You should ensure that you have adequate excess disposable income to service your loan repayments and to cope with an increase in your loan repayments if interest rates were to rise. You should also consider taking out appropriate insurance, particularly income protection, so that if you are unable to work due to accident or illness, you can still service the loan repayments and not be forced to sell the asset.

Positive, Neutral and Negative Gearing

Gearing may be classified into three levels – positive, neutral and negative. The category your geared investment falls into is determined by how much interest you pay on the loan, compared with how much income your investment earns.

For example, let's say you invest $150,000 in a parcel of shares, of which $100,000 is borrowed. The interest on your loan is 5% per annum or $5,000 in repayments.

> **Positive Gearing** - If the share portfolio produces income of $5,500, you will achieve a net cash flow gain of $500.

> **Neutral Gearing** - If the share portfolio produces income of $5,000, there is no net cash flow gain or loss.

> **Negative Gearing** - If the managed fund produces income of $4,500, you'll see a net cash flow loss of $500. This is the riskiest of gearing strategies and needs to be properly planned and considered.

GOALS

> *'Setting goals is the first step in turning the invisible into the visible'*
> *– Tony Robbins* (Tony Robbins on Quotlr, Life-Changing Quotes to Unleash Your Potential, 2024)

Defining your goals gives you a clear direction and picture of what you need to do to get where you need to be. ☺

Financial goals can generally be divided into three broad categories:

Short-term *0-2 years* – This may be a new car or your next holiday.
Medium-term *2-5 years* – You want to take an extended overseas trip or a put a deposit on a mortgage.
Long-term *5 years or more* - Major home renovations or retirement.

It helps to write down what you want to achieve over each of these periods and to set a specific deadline for each goal. This focuses your mind as well as your financial strategy.

To determine your deadlines, you will need to know:

- what your goals are,
- what you've already saved, and
- what is a realistic time frame to reach your goals.

Once your goals are clear, the next step is to work out what you need to do to reach them. Is it developing a budget, spending less, savings more, putting an investment in place, or striving for another job? Whatever it is, this is your path to achieving your goals.

ACTION: Access the Goals Map at our website: www.yourfinancialuniverse.com.au. Writing things down also helps keep us accountable!

REAL LIFE FINANCIAL UNIVERSES - Each of the case studies talks about setting some goals and how different individuals set themselves up to achieve them as much as possible.

GOVERNMENT

Australia is a democracy based on the British (Westminster) system of government, with the Governor-General the figurehead representing the King as part of the Commonwealth. In practice, all citizens over the age of 18 vote who will form government and govern the country. The main parliamentary parties are Liberal, Labour and The Greens. The party voted into the House of Representatives is led by the Prime Minister and they are responsible for governing the country and enacting legislation for new rules and regulations and for managing government services such as Medicare.

'The Australian Constitution is the set of rules by which Australia is run. The Constitution describes the structure, role and powers of the Australian parliament. It sets out how the Australian and state parliaments share the power to make laws' (Parliamentary Education Office, Australian Constitution, 2024).

GST – GOODS AND SERVICES TAX

The Goods and Services Tax (GST) was introduced in Australia on 1 July 2000 to consolidate and replace many of the federal wholesale and state taxes and make the tax system more streamlined whilst raising tax revenue for the government. When purchasing goods and services, 10% tax is applied on the price, and then it is paid to government by the supplier. GST is applied on most goods and services sold or consumed in Australia, with some exceptions such as some food and health care items.

H

HECS-HELP

The Australian government offer Commonwealth-supported places at tertiary institutions that are eligible for HECS-HELP loans. These loans assist students to pay their student contribution amount for their chosen degree, rather than having to pay in full up front (Department of Education, HELP, 2024).

The government and student contribution levels vary according to the university course chosen, with courses such as education and health receiving a higher level of government support. There is also a HELP loan limit that is applied, which is the maximum amount that a person can borrow. This also varies according to the study area; however, for most students is around $120,000. All rates and loan amounts are indexed regularly by the government.

Your HELP debt is repaid through the Australian Tax Office (ATO), and there are two ways that you can repay your loan:

1. **Compulsory Repayments** – These are taken directly out of your income once you earn above a certain level. You must advise your employer that you have a HELP debt so that they can withhold the appropriate amount of money from your pay. No repayment is required until you reach the earning threshold. The current threshold is $51,550 for the 2023/24 financial year with a percentage rate of 1%. The more you earn, the higher the percentage taken out of your pay to repay your debt. This is capped at 10% once you are earning over $151,000.

2. **Voluntary Repayments** – You can make a voluntary repayment at any time out of your own money, over and above any compulsory payments.

It is really important that you understand your entitlements and how much your degree is going to cost you! The StudyAssist website is a very useful resource that provides information on government assistance for financing tertiary study:

https://www.studyassist.gov.au/paying-back-your-loan/loan-repayment

KEY TIP:

- If you are planning to defer or considering changing courses, make sure you do so before the census date to avoid having to pay fees.
- If you are not sure about what course you want to study, then think about waiting or deferring. Your HELP debt will continue to grow regardless of whether you like what you are studying or not!
- Every course unit that you complete contributes to your HECs/HELP loan limit so if you change direction or courses multiple times you may have to fund some of the degree out of your own pocket!
- Consider that courses such as medicine have a low government contribution and so will cost you significantly more.
- There are also fees that are charged by the tertiary provider such as the Student Services and Amenities fees, usually about $350 per year, that must be paid out of your own pocket.

HEALTH INSURANCE

In Australia, private health insurance allows you to be treated in hospital as a private patient. It can also help pay for health care costs that Medicare doesn't cover. The government encourages individuals to take out private health insurance to take the pressure off the public Medicare system through measures such as:

- An additional Medicare levy surcharge on higher-income earners without private health insurance, and
- Lifetime health cover which encourages people to take out private health insurance at a younger age (before the age of 30) and maintain their cover. You are penalised with a 2% loading each year you delay taking out the cover.

Private health insurance can be taken out for **hospital cover** as a patient in either a public or private hospital, and **extras** which provide cover for things such as physiotherapy and dental.

KEY TIP: *You don't have to take out both hospital and extras covers with the same provider! This may end up being cheaper as well as providing more tailored cover to your needs.*

HOME LOAN

A home loan helps fund the cost of buying a property. You borrow the money from a bank or lender and use that money to purchase a home. You are required to then repay the amount back over a set period of time, usually between 20 to 30 years. The repayments and interest rate will be set at the start of the loan.

RELATED TOPICS
I – Interest Rates
M - Mortgage

INCOME

Income is the return you receive for working (salary) or from investments. Income received through working, employment or running a business is classified as **active income**. On the other hand, **passive income** is generated from investments without direct input, such as dividends received from a shareholding.

INTEREST RATES

Interest rates are two-fold:

- Interest rates are the cost you pay for borrowed money or credit, for example interest repayments on your mortgage; and
- Interest rates are the return you receive on your cash and fixed-interest investments, for example 3.5% per annum for a term deposit at the bank.

Economically, generally what happens when money is 'cheap' or interest rates are low, people and businesses tend to borrow more as less of their income needs to be directed to repay their debt. This generates spending and activity in the economy. On the other hand, as interest rates rise, more money needs to be directed to loan repayments and people and business have less to spend in the economy. This will 'slow down' economic activity. Interest rates can be fixed or variable:

- **Fixed interest** rates are set at the time of taking out a loan or investment and remain 'fixed' for the term of that loan or investment. Fixed interest rates may be beneficial for budgeting as the loan repayments won't change over time. If you have fixed interest investment, the income is reliable as it will remain at the same rate.
- **Variable interest** rates change with any interest rate changes made by the Reserve Bank of Australia. This means that the rate can move up or down over time. We have

recently encountered an ongoing period of rising interest rates which has meant that loan repayments for people with variable loans have significantly increased. On the other hand, should interest rates decline, the variable interest rates will also decline and in turn so will loan repayments.

INFLATION

Inflation is the rate at which prices rise. The most common way that inflation is measured is via the **Consumer Price Index** (CPI). The CPI measures changes in prices by comparing the price of a basket of goods and services purchased in one period with the same basket of goods and services in the next. If the basket costs more then there is inflation (increasing prices), which means you need to spend more money to buy the same basket of goods and services.

The Reserve Bank of Australia monitors inflation closely with a target of between 2% and 3% per annum.

INVESTMENT

According to Investopedia, 'an investment is an asset or item acquired with the goal of generating income or appreciation. Appreciation refers to an increase in the value of an asset over time. When an individual purchases a good as an investment, the intent is not to consume the good but rather to use it in the future to create wealth' (Investopedia, Investment Basics Explained, 2024).

RELATED TOPICS
A – Asset Classes
C - Compounding

Investments can take many forms, and we have covered the key assets that are used for investing earlier in this book. The importance of investments is that they are vehicles for building wealth.

ACTION: *Your Financial Universe checklist (at the end of the book; see page 131) gives you some options if you want to start investing. There are lots of ways you can begin, such as:*

- *A high interest earning account*
- *A share portfolio*

INSURANCE

Insurance deals with uncertainty concerning the occurrence of loss. By taking out an insurance policy, you transfer the risk of loss to an insurance company. Depending on the level and type of cover, you pay a premium to the insurance company for them to take on the risk of loss.

There are many different types of insurance within two key categories:

General insurance insures physical assets such as home and contents and motor vehicles.

Life insurance insures against life events such as premature death (life insurance) or an inability to earn an income (income protection).

Insurance premiums are set depending on your age, gender, health, house location, car storage or occupation, depending on the type of insurance. One way to affect the cost of insurance is using an **excess.** This lowers your regular premium; however, if you claim on your insurance, for example you have a car accident, you must pay the excess first before the insurer will repair your car. An excess can range from $200 up to $1,500 depending on the policy.

One of the most expensive insurances faced by young adults is car insurance. This is because the statistics show that people under the age of 25 are more often involved in motor vehicle accidents.

I

ACTION: *Think about whether you may need insurance and weigh up the cost with the risk. Replacing a house in the event of fire is a much more significant cost than replacing a gold ring.*

Consider your own position and ask questions such as:

- If my home or contents were lost in a fire, do I have the funds to rebuild/replace?
- If my car was stolen, what would be the implications? Would I need to replace the car, for example, for work purposes? Could I afford to do so?
- What would happen if I was not able to work for a period of time? Would I be able to pay my debt, fund my lifestyle, look after my family?

Every situation is different, and insurance can be expensive, particularly as you get older. Think about what losses would affect you, how would you deal with them, and the level of impact it would have on your everyday life. This will give you a good guide as to whether insurance may provide a solution to addressing the uncertainty of loss.

J

JOINT TENANCY

When you own a property with someone else, you can choose the ownership structure. The most common ownership is a **joint tenancy**. This means that you own the property equally with another person listed on the property title. This is a common structure when spouses or partners buy a property together. With this structure there are also implications on death, as the remaining share of the property automatically goes to the surviving owner.

In contrast, property owned as **tenants-in-common** means that each owner has a defined share of the property and holds it as their own. The shares do not need to be equal. This ownership structure has different consequences on death, as the distribution of the remaining share of the property is not automatic. Each tenant-in-common can determine to whom their share of the property goes or whether it is sold. This is a more common form of ownership structure for investment properties or family-owned properties (such as those owned between siblings) (Willed, Joint Tenancy vs Tenancy in Common: Property Ownership in Australia, 2024).

K

KNOWLEDGE

There is an old adage that 'Knowledge is power'. And when it comes to your finances, there is nothing truer.

Taking the time to educate yourself and increase your financial literacy will set you up for success! By understanding the economic and financial environment and your own finances, you will have more control over your wealth, which gives you more choices about your lifestyle, the way you want to live and what you want to do. Financial stress is a terrible feeling and is known to lead to other health issues both physical and mental.

Reading this book is a very healthy first step. ☺

LEVERAGE

Leverage is 'the act of using borrowed money to buy an investment (Cambridge Dictionary, 2024). The intention is that the value of the investment or asset will provide profits (both income and capital growth) that outweigh the interest paid on the borrowings.

Leverage allows you to **boost** your investment output.

Consider the following example:

	LEVERAGE	NO LEVERAGE
Borrowings	$400,000	$0
Your contribution	$100,000	$100,000
Total Asset purchase	$500,000	$100,000
Loan to value ratio = value of your loan / value of your investments.	$400,000 / $500,000 80%	0%
The asset appreciates **6%** per annum over **10 years:**		
End Value of Asset	**$895,423**	**$179,084**
	Repay $400,000 then increase in value is $395,423	**Increase in value is $79,084**

Using leverage **magnifies** the results; however, it is important that you only leverage what you can manage and is appropriate for your situation.

LINE OF CREDIT

A line of credit (LOC) is a preset borrowing limit that can be accessed and used at any time until the limit is reached. It is an arrangement between

RELATED TOPICS

G - Gearing
M - Mortgage

a lender (most commonly a bank) and a customer that establishes the maximum borrowing amount that can be accessed. Types of LOC include personal, business, and home equity. The main advantage with an LOC is the flexibility of having access to additional funds, and that you are only charged interest on the amount you use, not the entire borrowing limit. On the flip side, the interest rate may be higher than for a home mortgage for example, and there may be penalties for late payments (Investopedia, Line of Credit (LOC) Definition, 2024).

LIQUIDITY

Liquidity is the efficiency or ease with which an asset can be converted to cash without affecting its market price. The more liquid an asset is, the more quickly and easily the asset can be turned back into cash. Therefore, the most liquid asset is **cash** as it is readily available and can be used immediately. Contrast this to a property. If you need extra cash, you can't just sell a bathroom or a bedroom, and to sell the entire property takes time and involves costs such as agent fees. Generally, the proceeds from selling shares are available after three business days.

Liquidity is important to consider so that you don't tie up too much of your money in assets that are more difficult to sell and convert to cash. As they say, 'cash is king', so it's important to make sure you have enough in reserve!

RELATED TOPICS

G - Gearing
I - Interest Rates
M - Mortgage

LOAN

A loan is an amount of money that is borrowed and is expected to be paid back with interest. Loans can take many forms such as home, personal and business, and money can be borrowed from different lenders such as banks, credit unions or between people or businesses. The lender sets the conditions of the loan such as the interest rate and term.

M

MANAGED FUND

A managed fund pools the money of individual investors with a fund manager who then invests the money on behalf of those investors. Managed funds often invest in one particular asset class such as Australian shares, or alternatively across a range of asset classes such as fixed interest, shares and property. These often have labels based on the asset allocation such as *Conservative*, with a higher allocation to income-based assets such as bonds or *Growth*, which have a higher allocation to growth assets such as Australian and international shares.

The fund manager invests the pooled funds of investors and issues units in the fund. Each unit represents an equal portion of the fund's total value and the number of units you receive depends on how much money you invest. This means that you do not own any of the underlying assets in the fund, just units in the fund. Usually, the fund manager will charge an investment fee for their services in managing the fund; this fee is deducted from your investment total at regular periods (Australian Stock Exchange, Managed Funds, 2024).

If the underlying assets earn dividends or interest, the fund manager may distribute income to unit holders. When the underlying assets grow in value, the overall value of the fund also grows and therefore your unit price will increase. This provides investors with capital growth.

Managed funds are an easy way to invest as you get access to a broad range of different investments in one holding, as well as access to investments that may not be as accessible to the public. One thing to note with managed funds is that they may not be as liquid as other diversified options such as ETFs. This is because you must redeem your units first and then the fund manager sells down the necessary underlying investments to pay out your units. In some cases, this may take some time depending on how easy the underlying investments are to sell and how large the fund is.

MARGIN LENDING

A margin loan allows you to borrow money for an investment in shares or exchange traded funds (ETFs). With this type of loan, you contribute a percentage of the funds, and the lender contributes a percentage of the funds to purchase an investment. The key difference between a margin loan and a normal mortgage is that the loan must remain at a certain loan-to-value ratio (LVR) below an agreed level, most commonly 70%.

Loan-to-value ratio = value of your loan / value of your investments.

The LVR changes with the value of your investments. If your investments fall in value then your loan gets larger; if your investments increase in value then your loan reduces in value. If your investments fall below the agreed LVR than you will receive a margin call. A margin call means that you must get your LVR back to the agreed value.

To lower your LVR back to the agreed level, you have different options: deposit money into your account to reduce your margin loan balance; add more of your own existing shares to increase your portfolio value; or sell part of your portfolio and pay off your loan balance.

Margin loans are considered a higher-risk investment, because if the market or your shares take a significant market downturn then you can lose a lot more that you invest. Also, if you can't lower your LVR, the margin lender is able to sell some of your investments at the market value to lower your LVR. Most lenders will give you 24 to 48 hours to lower your LVR (Moneysmart, Borrowing to Invest 2024).

MEDICARE

The government Medicare system provides universal basic public hospital and medical cover to all Australian residents, including a wide range of health and hospital services at no or low cost. Medicare is funded by taxpayers via a special levy and the general tax system. All taxpayers, except those on low incomes, pay a levy of 2% on their taxable income.

You need to enrol for Medicare. When you turn 15 you can register for your own Medicare card or nominate to stay on your parents' card. You can enrol online here: Enrolling in Medicare - Medicare - Services Australia.

Medicare gives you access to free or lower-cost:

- medical services by doctors, specialists and other health

professionals. Some doctors may bulk bill, in which case you won't have to pay for anything.

- hospital treatment in a public hospital
- many prescription medicines
- mental health care

To encourage people to opt into the private health insurance system, the government imposes an additional levy on singles who earn more than $90,000 and couples and families with a combined taxable income of more than $180,000. They pay an additional Medicare Levy Surcharge (MLS) of between 1% and 1.5% depending on their income level.

KEY TIP: *If you are at the income level where the levy is charged, you need to consider whether you are better off obtaining health insurance. For example, if you are a single person earning $100,000 per annum you will be paying an additional surcharge of $1,000 per annum. Instead, you could direct that money to health insurance and receive all the benefits that are offered by having private health insurance, rather than paying an additional tax!*

Another initiative to encourage people to take up private health insurance at a younger age and to reward people who maintain continuous private health insurance was the introduction of Lifetime Health Cover which started on 1 July 2000. Under Lifetime Health Cover, people who join a health fund before they turn 30, and who keep their membership, will pay lower premiums than people who delay joining until they are older. People over the age of 30 pay a 2% loading on top of the base rate premium for each year they delay joining a private health fund (Health Direct, What Is Medicare?, 2024).

MINDFUL MONEY

Being mindful of our relationship with money is very important to our financial well-being and understanding financial stress. The way we **feel** about money and the **emotions** that we associate with money will impact our spending and saving habits.

Do we have a bad day and get online to make a new purchase that makes us feel happy and erases the 'bad' from our day? How do we feel about that purchase one minute, one hour, one day later? Has it still made us feel better?

Do we save our pennies for a rainy day that may never come? Do we not experience life as we want to because we are worried about not having enough money? Did we watch our parents spend their money and suffer financially so we want to make sure we have enough of a nest egg?

Whatever your relationship with money, as long as you recognise it, you can understand and change it, and for most of us it's finding balance. No **one** way of dealing with your financial situation is the right way. You need to find the right way for you so that you can eliminate financial stress but enjoy life to the fullest. It often goes back to our goals again. What do we want to achieve and how can we get there?

REAL LIFE FINANCIAL UNIVERSES

- *Each of the case studies shows how at different times in your financial life, you have different priorities and different thoughts about money and financial goals.*

MOBILE PHONE PLANS

There are so many options for mobile phone plans and sometimes it is hard to know which is the best value for money that meets your needs. There are two key types of plans available in Australia, prepaid and postpaid plans.

Prepaid plans are prepaid at the start of each month so that you pay for your mobile plan upfront before you've used any of it. Note that prepaid plans don't come with the phone so you will need to own the phone before signing up for a prepaid plan.

Postpaid plans are like a regular bill whereby you pay at the end of the month for your mobile usage after you have used the plan. Postpaid plans allow you to buy a phone, so if you are after the latest phone postpaid plans are the way to go! **Be wary though, as the latest phones are usually the most expensive and can significantly increase your monthly bill.**

Some of the comparison sites such as Canstar are a good starting point to consider the right plan for you. Some of the things to look out for include:

- How long will any plan discounts go for and what is the standard price once the discount has finished?
- How much data will you receive, and will it be enough for your needs?
- Is it easy to swap deals or providers? There is enough competition so you should not feel 'locked in'.
- Do you need the phone or just the SIM? Some providers may be better for phone and SIM deals rather than SIM only.

You can access Canstar Blue as a starting point here: https://www.canstarblue.com.au/phone/

MONETARY POLICY

Monetary policy is the responsibility of the Reserve Bank of Australia (RBA). Their focus is on an economy that is growing positively over time with low inflation (between 2% and 3% per annum). Their main tool to influence the economy and achieve these objectives is by adjusting interest rates.

As highlighted in the interest rates section, interest rates reflect the cost of money. When the RBA increases interest rates, it leaves less money in households' pockets as they need to spend more on their borrowings such as the mortgage. Therefore, they have less to spend in the economy on goods and services. The intention of this measure is to slow down the economy and bring down inflation, known as **monetary contraction**.

At the time of writing in 2024, we are in a period of rising interest rates and there have been 12 interest rate increases since May 2022. The intention is to reduce spending and bring down inflation, which hit its highest annual level since 1990, of 6.6% in 2022 (RateInflation, Australia Historical Interest Inflation Rates – 1948 to 2024, July 31, 2024).

In contrast if the economy needs to be stimulated, the RBA may decrease interest rates so that we need to direct less money to our debt repayment, leaving us more money to spend in the economy. This is known as **monetary expansion**. When there is more money in the economy generally this will fuel growth and business investment, for example, businesses hiring more staff to meet the increased demand.

MORTGAGE

Most people refer to their home loan as their mortgage, the loan being used to finance the purchase of a home. The mortgage itself is 'a conveyance of an interest in real property as security for the repayment of money borrowed to buy the property; a lien or claim on property such that the lender can take possession if the loan is not repaid' (Dictionary.com, 2024). This means that your **lender** can use your property as collateral should you fail to repay your home loan. It acts as their safety net for getting their money back! However, it also means that **you** can have the benefit of using your house as collateral for other lending, such as for home renovations or an investment.

RELATED TOPICS
I – Inflation
I – Interest Rates

MYGOV AND MYGOVID

myGov is a government portal that allows you to access different government services such as Centrelink, Medicare and the

Australian Tax Office from the one central website. Once you have created your own myGov login you can update your personal details, and link the services that you need to allow you to easily access these online, including when you are overseas, from the one login.

RELATED TOPICS
G – Gearing
H – Home Loan
M – Mortgage

To enhance the security of your personal information and your myGov account, the government has also created **myGovID**, which is your digital identity. This 'makes it easier to prove who you are online' (Australian Government, myGovID Home, 2024).

The government has recently changed the name of myGovID to myID. It operates the same way, just a different name.

KEY TIP: Create your own myGov login by scrolling down the page to 'Create a myGov account at the following website:

Sign in with myGov - myGov

To set up myGovID, you need to download the app and provide identification. To get started and understand what you need, head to the following website:

How to set up | myGovID

N

NASDAQ

The NASDAQ is a trading system that is commonly referred to in the media. It is based in New York and like the Australian Securities Exchange (ASX), it is a global electronic marketplace for buying and selling securities. It operates across 29 markets and most of the world's largest technology stocks are listed on the NASDAQ, including Apple (Investopedia, What NASDAQ Is, 2024).

The term NASDAQ is often used to refer to the NASDAQ composite which is an index of more than 2,500 stocks listed on the NASDAQ exchange. Some of the more familiar names incorporated in the index include Apple, Amazon, Microsoft and Tesla.

NET

Often used in financial information and when returns are quoted, is the term **net**. This simply refers to the figure remaining after elements such as taxes and fees have been incorporated.

For example, your net salary is your salary after tax and superannuation contributions. The net return of a share or managed fund is the return after all fees such as the management expense ratio and performance fees. Essentially it is the real return and is the amount you will actually receive.

○

OFFSET VERSUS REDRAW

An **offset account** is a transaction account that is linked to your home loan. The benefit of setting up an offset account is that it reduces the interest payable on your home loan. This is because the interest is calculated on the net balance, that being the mortgage amount less the balance in your offset account. Offset accounts work more like a transaction account and the funds are easily accessible.

A **redraw account** sits side-by-side with your home loan and allows you to make additional payments on your loan into the redraw account. These funds can be accessed when you need, for example, to pay for home renovations; however in general they do not work as an everyday account like an offset. Similar to an offset account, however, is that the interest is calculated on the net balance, that being the mortgage amount less the balance in your redraw facility (Moneysmart.gov.au, 2024).

Different lenders offer different types of lending and loan account facilities, so choose one that better suits your need. For example, if you want your extra loan repayments to be less accessible, then a redraw account may be a better option.

P

POWER OF ATTORNEY

A power of attorney is a legal document where one person (the 'donor') appoints another person (the 'attorney') to act on their behalf. This provides for situations where the donor is incapable of acting. This might be because of an extended overseas trip or because of illness that prevents full participation in managing affairs. The person appointed as an attorney must be able to be trusted completely and a trusted friend or family member is a common choice.

There are three basic types of powers of attorney depending on the situation for which it is required.

- **General Power of Attorney** is usually put in place to give an attorney power to act in a specific situation or for a set period of time, for example purchasing a house or acting on someone's behalf when they are on an extended overseas holiday. A general power of attorney lapses if the person who has given the power of attorney becomes mentally incapable of managing their own affairs.
- **Enduring Power of Attorney** continues beyond the donor's loss of mental capacity. This allows the attorney to continue acting, even though the donor has lost their mental capacity. This is put in place so that there is someone who can act on your behalf if something happens to you and you are unable to make your own decisions. These are often put in place between spouses or partners.
- **Medical Power of Attorney** is put in force to authorise someone to make decisions regarding the donor's medical treatment when they are unable to do so for themselves.

It is important to consider how your affairs would be managed if you were unable to act. Powers of attorney laws and requirements also vary between states, so it is important that you consult a legal practitioner before putting these in place.

PRESENT VALUE

Present value (PV) is the current value of a future sum of money or income flow, given a specified rate of return. This may sound a bit complicated, but the key to understanding present value is the assumption that a dollar today is worth more than the same dollar in the future. If you want to save and not spend your dollar, you want to achieve a 'return' on your dollar as reward for not spending. This is the interest rate or dividend of a share, for example. Understanding present value is important if we want to compare values over time.

The formula is as follows:

Present Value = Future Value / (1 + rate of return) number of payment periods.

Let's say you expect to receive $50,000 ten years from now with an annual rate of return of 5%.

Present Value = $50,000 / (1 + 0.05) 10 = $30,695.66. The expected $50,000 is worth $30,695.66 in today's money.

It is also useful if you are given an option to receive a different amount of money now or in the future. Using the present value formula, you can work out which will be the better alternative (Investopedia.com, What Is Present Value in Finance and How Is It calculated, 27 June 2024).

PRINCIPAL

The principal of a loan is simply the **total amount** you borrow from a lender. This is the amount on which interest will subsequently be paid.

RELATED TOPICS
G – Gearing
H – Home Loan
M – Mortgage

PROFIT

Profit is the amount of money or income that remains after considering expenses such as operating costs, taxes and debts. Profit is often used as a measure of the success and feasibility of a company and can be distributed by companies to their shareholders in the form of dividends.

In contrast to profit is revenue. Revenue is the amount of income generated by business operations such as the sale of goods or services. Revenue is the 'raw' figure and doesn't take into account the costs that are associated with generating the revenue.

Q

QUALITY OF LIFE

Quality of life means different things to different people, and how your financial position fits in with that is an individual choice. Your financial position is only one part; health, work life balance and family considerations are also factors related to one's quality of life.

ACTION: What does quality of life mean for you? How do your finances fit in and work towards your idea of quality of life?

Consider your own position and ask questions such as:

- Is travel important for life enjoyment and experience? If so you may want to set up an automatic transfer from your wages to a separate 'travel' account.
- Is work-life balance important? If so, you may accept a lower salary or lower-pressure job to achieve flexibility and balance.

R

RATE OF RETURN (REAL VERSUS GROSS)

'The rate of return (RoR) is used to measure the profit or loss of an invest-ment over time' (Investopedia, Rate of Return (ROR) Meaning, Formula and Examples, July 20, 2024).

It is important to understand the difference between the real rate of re-turn and the simple rate of return. When the gross (sometimes referred to as simple) rate of return is calculated it does not take into account the effects of inflation, and is calculated with reference to the investment balance:

$$RoR = \frac{\text{Current Value - Initial Value}}{\text{Initial Value}} \times 100$$

For example, if we invest $10,000 and it grows to $13,000 over time, the RoR is

$$\frac{13{,}000 - 10{,}000}{10{,}000} = 30\%$$

We know inflation eats into the value of money over time, so using the real rate of return takes into account the effects of inflation. This can be particularly important as when inflation is high (such as 7%) this erodes the real value of our investment return over that period.

Using the above example, if there was 7% inflation over the same investment period, the real return is reduced to 23%.

REAL ESTATE

Real estate refers to general property. This can be any type of property, including residen-

RELATED TOPICS
I – Inflation

tial, commercial or retail, but includes both the permanent structure and the land itself. The key element of real estate is the **LAND!** Land is the real value that you purchase as this is what will increase or decrease in value over time. In general, the buildings and structures on top of the land will depreciate.

The value of land is a much researched and documented concept, but it is important to understand that this is what drives prices of real estate. Land is a **finite** resource. As Mark Twain said, 'Buy land, they're not making it any more'.

There are some essential elements that drive the value of the land, such as location, level of infrastructure and population growth. So, if you are buying a property, try to actively consider the long-term land value. Would people prefer to live in an area that has good infrastructure such as retail precincts, good road networks and public transport? Is the area going to develop as our population increases? These factors contribute to whether the LOCATION is the right one and the true VALUE of that land.

The concept of the *Law of Economic Rent* explains why land prices continually increase over time and how the 'rent' from the land is captured. There are many better scholars on this topic than me and many books that have been written that not only discuss the value and power of the land but also the economic cycles that drive its value. There are two particular books by Phil Anderson and Akhil Patel (as noted in the Bibliography) that are well worth reading if you are interested in further understanding the importance of land values in our economy.

RENT

Rent is the money that is paid by the tenant to live in or occupy a property. The rent is paid to the owner of the property as the 'price' for letting the tenant have use of the property.

There is much debate about whether renting or buying is a better option financially. This may purely be a financial decision and based on your own personal circumstances or depend on what is happening in the market. When there is a shortage of rental properties for example, this pushes up the price of rent and rent may be a higher expense than making mortgage repayments.

There are many considerations and pros and cons for renting, including:

- By renting you may be able to live where you want to if you can't afford to buy where you would ideally like to live.
- You may live in a better house than you could afford to buy, and you are not limited by the amount you can borrow.
- You don't have the transaction costs. There are many costs that come with buying, selling and maintaining a property.
- The flip side of renting is that you are at the mercy of your landlord. We've all heard stories of horrible land-lords who are not responsive to fixing broken taps or maintaining the property at the expected standard.
- The amount you have to pay will change, and you need to factor in rent increases.
- You may have to move when you don't want to. Packing up and moving house takes a lot of energy and time.

There is also another option: **RENTVESTING**. This is a strategy where you purchase a property that you don't live in. This may be a valid option if you can't afford to buy where you want to live, but it allows you to enter the property market at some level. Further, the best place to buy a property for long-term growth and rental prospects may not be the place you want to live. You may want to invest interstate where growth in infrastructure and population may be better and therefore the rental income AND growth opportunities are higher.

It must be considered that you will also become a landlord. This may not be for everyone! In addition there will be costs associated with investment property ownership such as land tax and tax implications.

KEY TIP: *With property prices on the increase around Australia, rentvesting is a very credible strategy that allows you to get into the market at a level you can afford. Do your homework on the area where you are planning to buy, understand the impacts on your cash flow and tax position and if necessary seek out expert advice so that you can make an informed decision.*

RISK

Risk, according to the Oxford Dictionary, is 'the possibility of something bad happening at some time in the future; a situation that could be dangerous or have a bad result' (Oxford Learner's Dictionary, Oxford University Press, 2024).

Risk is therefore based on the concept of uncertainty, and in financial / investment terms it relates to the 'chance that an outcome or investment's actual gains will differ from an expected return'. That risk can relate to one of the following:

- The original value of your investment goes down and you lose some or all of your original investment;
- Your investment doesn't provide the return you expected and/or needed; or
- Your investment returns a lower income than expected; for example you receive a lower share dividend than anticipated.

In general, the higher the risk, the higher the possible return needs to be as the investor needs to be rewarded for taking on an additional risk. For example, if I put my money in a bank, that is much safer than investing in a new technology stock. Because of that additional risk I would expect that the technology stock provides a higher level of reward or return to compensate me for taking on that additional risk.

The level of risk we can accept may also be related to time horizon and liquidity needs:

- If we need our money to be easily accessible, we are much less likely to invest in a high-risk investment or one that is difficult to access or takes time to liquidate.
- If we have a longer time horizon, we may be more willing to invest in higher-risk assets as we have time to ride out the volatility or ups and downs of that investment and in turn achieve higher returns. An older retired investor will need at least a portion of their investments to be easily accessible to provide them with their on-going income needs. They will need to invest some of their portfolio in lower-risk, more liquid investments.

RELATED TOPICS
A – Asset Classes
A – Asset Allocation
I - Insurance

We also previously discussed the impact of risk in our everyday lives and whether we need to insure against that risk, for example taking out life insurance to protect our family in the event of premature death.

RISK PROFILE

An investment risk profile is an assessment of an 'individual's willingness and ability to take risks' (Investopedia, Risk Profile: Definition, 2024). The appropriate investment asset allocation should be based on your risk profile. If you are comfortable with taking on higher risks, investment in growth assets such as shares and property can be a large part of your portfolio. In contrast, if you are inexperienced or nervous about investing, a lower risk profile and investment in assets such as fixed interest and cash may be more appropriate.

It is important that you select the right risk profile for you – one that can achieve your objectives and one that allows you to sleep at night! There is no point in investing in a portfolio that makes you uncomfortable and nervous.

Risk profiles tend to be broken into categories with labels that indicate the types of investments that would be incorporated into the port-folio. Examples include low risk, conservative, balanced, aggressive and high growth.

RELATED TOPICS
A – Asset Classes
A – Asset Allocation

These types of labels and portfolios are often used in superannuation funds and the investor selects the risk profile that they feel is appropriate for them. An example is the Balanced portfolio below, which has an asset allocation of approximately 70% growth assets and 30% income.

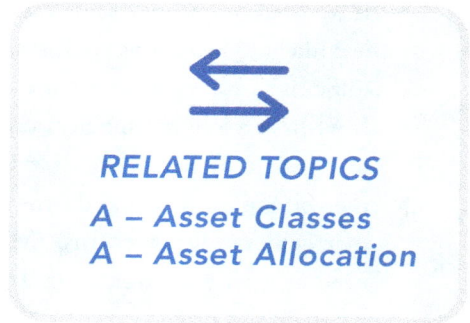

BALANCED

Strategic asset allocation

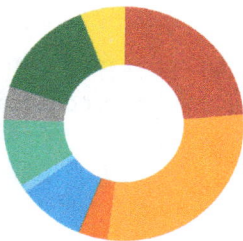

ASSET CLASS	RANGE	ALLOCATION
Australian shares	10-45%	23.5%
International shares	10-45%	28.5%
Private equity	0-15%	4%
Unlisted infrastructure	0-30%	9%
Listed infrastructure	0-10%	1%
Unlisted property	0-30%	8%
Listed property	0-10%	1.5%
Credit	0-20%	4.5%
Fixed interest	0-25%	14%
Cash	0-20%	6%
Other assets	0-5%	0%

Source: Hands-Off & Diversified Super Account | AustralianSuper

S

S&P INDICES

S&P (previously known as Standard and Poor's) is a global company that creates financial indices representing a variety of market subsets such as the Top 500 companies, commodities and sustainability.

One of the most known and quoted in the financial media is the S&P 500 index. This is a broad and diverse index of the Top 500 leading publicly traded US companies and is widely regarded as one of the best indicators of the US equities market.

SALARY

Salary refers to the wages or money that you are paid by your employer. This is a fixed, regular payment that is agreed on the commencement of your job. Your salary will be taxed depending on the level of your income.

In Australia, superannuation also forms part of your salary and is a mandatory payment that employers must make into your superannuation fund on your behalf.

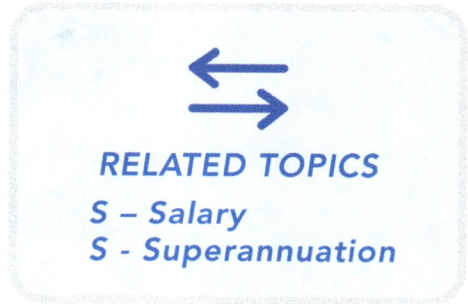

RELATED TOPICS
S – Salary
S - Superannuation

SHARES

Sometimes also referred to as stocks, equities or securities, **shares** are investments in businesses that are listed on a stock exchange. When you purchase a share, you are buying part of that company. For example, if I buy 10 ANZ shares I own a small piece of the ANZ company. My investment in ANZ may provide me an investment return in two different ways:

- **Capital Growth:** The price of the share goes up, which is a capital return or growth of my initial investment.
- **Income:** ANZ may issue a dividend to their shareholders, usually calculated as a percentage of their profits.

Often shares are categorised as either income or growth focused, and investors can choose shares that meet their investment objectives. For example, a speculative technology share will be growth focused with investors hoping that they are investing in the next Apple!

Australian shares are investments in companies that are listed on the Australian Stock Exchange (ASX). We can also invest in *international shares*. With technology and a global economy, we can purchase shares in the companies of many different countries ranging from those listed on the New York Stock Exchange through to the Tokyo Stock Exchange or even the National Stock Exchange of India. According to Statista, as at January 2023, the Australian stock market only made up 2.2% of the total world equity market value. International shares, therefore, offer lots of additional opportunities for growth and diversification across the globe.

SUPERANNUATION

Superannuation is money that is contributed by your employer into a separate fund as part of your salary. The **sole purpose** of superannuation is to save for your retirement so that when you retire, you have a pool of money to provide for your lifestyle and spending. From a government perspective, these 'forced' savings also reduce reliance on social welfare and pensions.

Employer superannuation contributions are mandatory, and the contribution rate was 11.5% as of 1 July 2024. This will increase to 12% on 1st July 2025. These contributions are taxed by the fund at 15% and this is considered a concessional rate of tax as it is lower than the first marginal tax bracket. Any earnings that the fund makes as you are accumulating superannuation are also taxed at 15%. When you take an income from superannuation on retirement, there is no tax on that income. This is a major incentive for people to contribute to their superannuation.

Superannuation is managed under a trust structure, so think of the fund as the house for your investments, it is not an investment in itself. The trustees of the fund have legislated responsibilities and must act in accordance with the trust deed, relevant legislation and in the BEST interests of members.

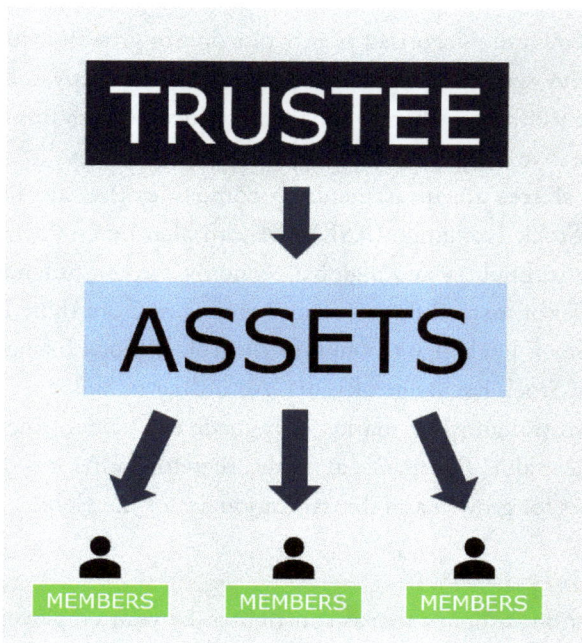

Contributions

Contributions into your superannuation fund are important to grow your superannuation balance. There are different ways that we can get money into our superannuation fund, the most common being via our employer. There are two key types of contributions:

Concessional Contributions – *These are contributions, including your employer's and any personal superannuation contributions such as salary sacrifice, that are taxed at the concessional rate of 15%. The current limit as at 1 July 2024 is $30,000 per annum for each individual.*

Non-concessional Contributions - *You can also make non-concessional contributions into your superannuation using after-tax funds, for example from savings in your bank account. From 1 July 2024, the non-concessional contributions cap is $120,000 per annum.*

Building your capital base through maximising your superannuation contributions is a key strategy for growing your superannuation balance up until retirement.

SUPERANNUATION FUND CHOICE

One of the key considerations for your superannuation is your choice of fund. Although retirement seems a long way away when you are younger, the fund and investment selection can make a big difference on your end balance. For many people, superannuation is their second biggest asset and yet as we do not 'see it' regularly we forget about it. Remember the power of compounding: that is what's happening with your superannuation. All of the returns stay in the fund and continue to grow. So it is important to have a good understanding of what your superannuation is doing for you! The importance of superannuation is intensified by the fact that we are living longer so our money needs to last longer!

There are so many options when it comes to choosing a superannuation fund, but these are the three key types of funds:

Industry – These were originally developed as funds to support trade union and industry bodies to provide for their members in retirement. These have grown significantly over time and are generally now available to anyone. Some of the biggest industry super funds include Australian Super, AWARE Super and HESTA. The biggest difference between an industry fund and a retail fund is that industry funds are not for profit and return any profit back to their members. They often have lower fees and generally a reduced number of investment options.

Retail – These are offered by financial services companies such as Colonial First State, MLC and Macquarie. These generally offer a large choice of investments but may have higher fees. Any profits generated by these funds go back to the company.

Self-Managed Superannuation Funds (SMSF)– A SMSF is a trust structure that is set up to manage assets for the benefit of its members (beneficiaries). These are used for people wanting more control over their superannuation assets and investments and the individuals themselves are the trustees of the fund. The trustees of the SMSF are legally liable for the running and administration of the fund and ensuring that it complies with both superannuation and tax rules, including lodgement of the Fund's annual return. SMSFs are suited to individuals with higher monetary balances (usually more than $500,000), a higher level of financial knowledge and the time and understanding to manage the fund in accordance with the regulations.

Getting the right fund for you is important and there are many resources on the internet that review superannuation funds, including the pros and cons of each.

Accessing your superannuation

In order to access your superannuation, you must meet a **condition of release**. The most common condition is when we retire or reach our preservation age. For most of us now our preservation age is 60 or above.

Your superannuation may also be accessed by meeting another condition of release such as being terminally ill or in severe financial hardship however these are very limited and have strict conditions that must be met.

Other 'super' facts:

- Many people have more than one super fund. If there isn't a reason for this (such as holding insurances), consider consolidating into one fund only. That way you are only paying one set of fees and one fund is much easier to manage.
- You can own insurances within your superannuation fund. Often these are default levels of insurance, such as death insurance, that you automatically receive when you join the fund. The premiums are deducted from your superannuation fund. If you need insurances, it can be a way of having insurances and not affecting

RELATED TOPICS
C - Compounding
S - Salary

your cash flow. Be mindful, however, that it does reduce your superannuation balance.

ACTION: *Who is your superannuation provider? How is it invested? Consider your superannuation position and ask yourself questions such as:*

- *What are the fees in my superannuation?*
- *Where is my superannuation invested? Do I need to change my asset allocation?*
- *Do I have insurance in my superannuation fund? Many people have insurance owned within their superannuation and do not realise they even have it!*

T

TAX AND THE INCOME TAX EQUATION

Income tax in Australia is based on a progressive tax system where the higher your earnings the higher the rate of tax that you pay. We also have a tax-free threshold where no tax is applied. When you join an employer, you will normally have to complete a tax declaration which allows your employer to deduct the tax amount directly from your wage. The employer then pays the tax to the Australian Taxation Office.

The current rates are shown in the Australian Tax Office schedule below:

Resident tax rates 2024–25

Taxable income	Tax on this income
0 – $18,200	Nil
$18,201 – $45,000	16c for each $1 over $18,200
$45,001 – $135,000	$4,288 plus 30c for each $1 over $45,000
$135,001 – $190,000	$31,288 plus 37c for each $1 over $135,000
$190,001 and over	$51,638 plus 45c for each $1 over $190,000

Source: Tax Rates – Australian Resident | Australian Taxation Office (ato.gov.au)

These rates do not include the **Medicare Levy** of 2%. Income tax is applied on all forms of income including salary and wages, rental income received from investment properties and dividends received from share investments.

Note that non-residents generally pay a higher level of tax and do not receive the tax-free threshold.

The tax rates can be updated by the government of the day passing new legislation and tax reduction is always a popular policy platform.

Lodging a Tax Return

In order for the government to ensure that people are paying the right amount of tax, most people who are earning an income will be required to lodge a tax return. A tax return will detail how much income you have earned in a financial year, less any tax deductions that you are entitled to. Tax deductions may apply to expenses that you incur when you are earning an income such as work-related car expenses.

The return must cover the tax year (financial year) between 1 July and 30 June. If you have paid too much tax you may be eligible for a refund of the extra tax. However, if you have not paid enough tax you may receive a tax bill. The tax office provides three key options as to how you can lodge your tax return:

- *Lodge your tax return online with myTax*
  Prepare and lodge your own tax return online. It is the quick, safe and secure way to lodge, most process in two weeks.
- *Lodge your tax return with a registered tax agent*
  Use a registered tax agent to prepare and lodge your tax return. They are the only people that can charge a fee.
- *Lodge a paper tax return*
  You can use the paper tax return to lodge your tax return by mail; most refunds issue within 50 business days (ATO, How to Lodge Your Tax Return, www.ato.gov.au, 2024).

There are lots of other taxes that we pay in everyday life, such as the **Goods and Services Tax (GST)**.

Companies pay a different rate of tax depending on their turnover. In general, companies with a total turnover of less than $50 million pay 25% tax on their earnings, with bigger companies earning above that level paying a higher level of 30% tax.

TAX FILE NUMBER

As part of the taxation requirements and to access the resident tax rates and tax-free threshold, you need to obtain a Tax File Number (TFN). This is your personal reference number that you retain for your lifetime in the tax and superannuation systems. It is a unique number to you and forms part of your identity, so make sure you keep it stored safely!

According to the ATO, you should 'only disclose your TFN to people and organisations that require it for legitimate reasons, such as:

- us – the Australian Taxation Office (ATO) – when discussing your tax records;
- your employer when you start work;
- your bank or financial institution;
- other government agencies to claim benefits;
- your superannuation fund; and
- your university' (ATO, What Is a Tax Fie Number, 2024).

You can apply for your Tax File Number online through the ATO here: Apply for a TFN | Australian Taxation Office (ato.gov.au)

TERM DEPOSIT

A term deposit is classified as a fixed interest investment. The investor deposits funds into a financial institution for a set period of time at a fixed interest rate. Terms usually range from one month through to three years and usually the longer the term, the higher the interest rate received. It is important that investors understand that the funds must remain invested for the nominated term; otherwise there is a termination penalty.

U

UNEMPLOYMENT

The unemployment rate is an important economic measure as there is a strong relationship between unemployment and economic growth (as measured by GDP). In times of economic growth, unemployment tends to be lower as there are more people engaged in working to create the growth in the economy.

The unemployment rate is calculated based on all Australian residents and is measured by the number of unemployed people divided by the total labour force (the sum of the unemployed and the employed). The unemployment rate is not a perfect measure and has some quirks such as 'employed' including people who are only part time or casual. These people may be employed but need more work. Usually therefore, the unemployment rate is considered a conservative estimate of the real unemployment rate. (Australian Bureau of Statistics, 2024)

UNSECURED DEBT

Unlike a home mortgage or an investment loan which is backed by the property or the investment, unsecured debt is not backed by any collateral or a guarantor (a person who agrees to pay the debt should the primary borrower not make the repayments as agreed) (LegalVision, What Are the Rights and Obligations of a Guarantor, 2020). The lender cannot take any of the borrower's property in the case of default, so it is far more risky for the lender. Interest rates on unsecured debt are usually higher than secured debt because of this additional risk. Some examples of unsecured debt include credit cards and personal loans.

V

VALUE OF MONEY

The value of money has been referred to in many different ways throughout this book. In the context of **inflation**, it refers to the way that increasing prices decrease the value of our money as a dollar tomorrow can't buy as much as a dollar today.

It's also a very personal trait as to how much we value money and whether we are savers or spenders and how important it is to **achieve our goals.**

Finally, it also refers to the fact that 'money is worth more now than at a future date based on its earning potential. Because money can grow when invested, any delay is a lost opportunity for growth' (Investopedia, Time Value of Money, 2024). This highlights again the importance of **compounding** and investing to earn a return. When we invest our $1,000 it can grow by earning interest and in three years it may be worth $1,300. If we

RELATED TOPICS
C – Compounding
G – Goals
I – Inflation

don't invest our $1,000 we've missed out on the extra $300 and we won't be able to buy as much with it due to inflation.

VOLATILITY

Volatility in investment terms refers to the up and down movement in the value of an investment, often unpredictably and quickly. For example, this may mean that you purchase a share for $10 then it drops in value to $2 then goes back up to $12. This is the risk that you take when purchasing the share. In general, higher volatility and large swings in value are associated with higher-risk assets such as international or speculative shares.

Volatility can be managed by diversifying your investments so that whilst one share may be taking a sharp drop, the remaining investments are relatively stable. Also, being able to hold onto assets over a longer time frame means that you can ride out the bumps without the need to sell or dispose of your investment at a low point in the market.

Making sure you are comfortable with the risk and volatility of your investments should be a key component of any investment strategy.

RELATED TOPICS

A – Asset Allocation

D – Diversification

R – Risk

W

WALL STREET

When you listen to the financial news you may hear the term 'Wall Street'. This has become the catch-all phrase 'for the financial markets of the United States as a whole, the American financial services industry, New York–based financial interests, or the Financial District itself' (Wikipedia, Wall Street, 2024).

The New York Stock Exchange building is on Wall Street; the Federal Reserve Bank and many financial firms and banks also call this area of Lower Manhattan home.

WILL

A will is a legal document that directs how your estate assets (things that you own) are to be distributed amongst your nominated beneficiaries (those who you would like to receive your money/assets).

As part of your will, you are required to nominate an executor. The executor has the duty of carrying out your wishes in your will and is granted power to administer the estate. Your executor should be someone you trust to act according to your wishes in the will.

Wills are important legal documents that can be prepared two ways:

- There are many online will kits available on the internet. These can cater for more simple wishes and situations.
- A solicitor is the best person to assist you with more complex scenarios, such as divorced spouses or where young children may need to be protected and/or provided for.

X

X MARKS THE SPOT!

In the treasure map of Life, **X** is where you want to be! What that looks like is up to you – financial freedom, your first house or travel! Set your goals and follow your dreams. We hope this book can help you get there! ☺

ACTION: Use the Goals Map to set yourself up to achieve your goals, both big and small. Access this at the Your Financial Universe website www.yourfinancialuniverse.com.au.

Y

YIELD

Yield, in finance terms, refers to the income that is generated by a particular investment, such as interest earned, or dividends received.

Z

ZOMBIE DEBT

'Zombie debt is debt that has fallen off your credit report but, for various reasons, someone is still trying to collect' (Adam Hayes, Investopedia, Zombie Debt: What It Means, How It Works, 2021). It will generally relate to debt that is more than three years old that has been forgotten about, belonged to someone else or has already been paid off.

Zombie debt may 'rise from the dead' as the original creditor to which the money is owed sells the debt to a debt collection agency. These agencies can be dogged in trying to retrieve the debt and getting you to pay and can make harassing and threatening phone calls. If you are subject to such an effort, make sure you know your rights in terms of the debt outstanding.

REAL LIFE
FINANCIAL
UNIVERSES

On the next few pages are some case studies about how other people have approached their finances at different stages of life and what they have learnt along the way.

Maybe some ideas relate to your own situation. Take what works and use it to your advantage and add it to your own plan.

I'M MOVING UP AND MOVING OUT - ALICE

Alice is 26 and has been working full time for about three years since obtaining her degree. She decided to move out when she was 25 years old and was feeling secure in her job and ready to gain some real independence. Here are Alices' thoughts on money and some of the challenges of moving out.

■ *How did you support yourself financially to make the move?*

I worked for 18 months full time before moving out. I also didn't have to pay for any rent or bills while living with my family so felt financially secure in my savings to be able to move out.

■ *What were the major costs for you in moving out of home? Were there any surprises?*

The major cost aside from rent was paying our bond. I moved in with two friends so that we could share the costs both upfront and ongoing. As a part of our lease agreement, we paid our bond which was over $1,000 each, and the first four weeks of rent upfront, so this was a significant initial outlay.

On top of this, we had to purchase some bits of furniture and household goods – even little things like food staples for the pantry all add up.

■ *Do you have any tips for someone saving to move out for the first time?*

Have a savings goal set before you move out to ensure you have a comfortable level of savings set aside. This will ease the adjustment of having such a large portion of your salary go towards living out of home expenses.

I would also recommend ensuring you are comfortable enough on your salary to be paying for living out of home expenses. If for any reason this will cause too much of a strain on your current and future savings, it is probably not the best time to move out and I would try to save more so that you can manage the upfront and ongoing expenses.

■ *Are you a spender or a saver? Explain why you categorise yourself like that!*

I would have to say I am a spender. When I was living at home, I found it a lot easier to save for things like overseas trips or big purchases as I had a lot more disposable income. Now that I live out of home, 40-50% of my pay goes to rent, bills and groceries. By the time I have set this money aside and put money aside for spending such as car insurance, gym membership and going out, I don't find that I have very much left over to save. Because of this, it can be hard to feel as though I'm getting ahead in my savings so sometimes it does feel a bit pointless. I do try to save something but recognise that I may have to wait until I am earning a higher salary.

■ *What's your definition of financial freedom?*

Financial freedom to me is earning a high enough salary that you can spend your finances freely, while also still contributing to your savings each pay cycle.

STARTING WORK - ANGUS

Angus started working at an early age and has tried to support himself as much as possible through school and now into university. He talks about what working part-time has meant to him and how he managed working with his study.

■ *What did you do for work when you were at school?*

During my final years of school, when I was studying VCE, I often tried to minimise my work just to weekends so that I could manage and focus on my studies. This would often be refereeing basketball games in the local domestic competition, something I had been doing since I was 15. I was also playing high-level sport so I had to balance my workload between sport, working and study. This sometimes meant forgoing earning money and reducing my spending.

■ *What age did you start working and where did you work?*

I started working when I was 9 years old. This was quite unofficial work, just helping out with coaching and the sausage sizzle at my local AFL AusKick on a Saturday morning. My dad was a lead coach, so he helped me get started with the job. It was very casual and good to start to earn my own money on the side of being a kid. Later, when I was 12, I started working at a café in the coastal town of Lorne. Our family often went there on holiday during the summer, so when I could, I would pick up shifts at the cafe. I was pretty much happy to do anything, from washing dishes, helping prepare milkshakes, juices and smoothies, and occasionally serve customers.

■ *How did you get to work?*

The first jobs that I had when I was younger, I would walk or ride my bike when they were close. Now that I have finished school and am heading to university I have my license. It's good because I can do a few different jobs and I currently work with an arborist, as well as coach and referee basketball. Driving and having more flexibility at university has helped me extend the amount of hours I can work per week.

■ *What was the main thing you spent your money on at school?*

My work whilst I was at school was pretty minimal so I earned about $100 to $200 per week. I was very cautious about my spending because it was a lot of effort to actually earn it. Most of my money was spent on going out, takeaway food and sometimes a nice dinner with my girlfriend. When I felt I had a bit of extra, I would sometimes splurge to buy a new pair of shoes or some clothes.

■ *Are you a spender or a saver? Explain why you categorise yourself like that!*

I would definitely describe myself as a saver. At the moment I have a rule, whatever money I make or get given, whether that's wages or birthday gifts, I try to save a minimum of 50%. I organise my bank account into three separate accounts: 'Money In', 'Savings' and 'Spending'. All of my wages and any transfers go straight into 'Money In', and from there I will transfer into each separate account. I have my accounts set up so that I can't transfer from my 'Savings' to 'Spending'. I find that this system holds me accountable and reduces my spending whilst still allowing me to splurge sometimes.

■ *What was a benefit of working part-time while you were at school?*

When working part-time at school, despite only making a small amount of ongoing money, I found that it allowed me to be semi self-sufficient and more independent as I had access to small sums of money that could get me by day to day when I needed it. When you are working you do appreciate the value of money more and what it takes to earn it! If I could go back I would probably try to work more when I was in younger year levels, such as grade 9 and grade 10.

■ *What's the one piece of financial knowledge that you wished you had earlier?*

I wish I had known and recognised how much our childhood is catered for by our parents and how a little bit saved early can go a long way. Children and teenagers are at an optimal point in life to save without having day-to-day living expenses, no bills, minimal tax, etc. I wish I had taken advantage of this further as a kid, working longer hours, picking up more jobs, in an effort to save more easily for my future.

■ *What's your definition of financial freedom?*

When I hear the words 'financial freedom', I straight away think to early retirement. I hope to be able to fund my lifestyle, whilst also giving back to the people who have helped me get to where I am, being mostly my parents. I believe financial freedom can be achieved from both hard work and also being smart with your money. At the moment I am trying to work quite long hours so that I can save more, and I have also started an investment portfolio. Together, I think this combination can be quite powerful financially in early adulthood.

BUYING OUR FIRST HOME - JACK & SOPHIE

Jack and Sophie are in their late twenties and have been married for almost two years. They spent some time living in Queensland before coming back to Melbourne to settle down. At age 28, they have recently purchased their first home. Here are some of Jack's thoughts on getting into the property market for the first time!

■ *When did you decide to buy your own home? What prompted the decision?*
Buying our own home was the next logical decision once Sophie and I got married, had spent a year living in Queensland and were moving back to Melbourne. We no longer wished to live in share houses, were keen to have a permanent home without needing to move in the next couple years and had the available funds to purchase our first home.

■ *Did you put in place a set savings plan to raise a deposit? Did you have a target in mind in terms of the percentage of deposit to borrowing?*
Yes, we are fairly careful about saving and calculating our money. Each fortnight we were paid we would deposit a fixed amount into a high-interest savings account. Initially we aimed for about 40% of our salaries; however, this amount fluctuated as our salaries changed and we had other expenses.

[Jack particularly had developed this habit and says he started as soon as he got his first full-time job, with the long-term goal of buying a house.]

We were firmly aiming to save a 20% deposit to avoid Lenders Mortgage Insurance (LMI). I read a Noel Whittaker book (given to me by Grandpa!) about the long-term savings associated with avoiding LMI. In the end though, our purchase was tied to other priorities such as the dates of us moving back to Victoria, and so we just focused on saving as much as we could before having to move back and look at buying our first house.

■ *What were the major costs for you in buying your first home? Were there any surprises?*
The home itself was the major cost, and of course stamp duty. We researched the other costs associated with purchasing property and found government websites helpful in indicating the other costs, such as conveyancing and building

inspection. One I was not aware of was having to purchase home insurance as a condition of the mortgage.

This was the website we used: https://www.vic.gov.au/first-home-buyer-guide

■ **Did you have to compromise on what home you bought?**

We set ourselves a few 'ideals' that we were looking out for such as location, proximity to our friends and family, and access to public transport. We were prepared to make concessions depending on the property as we were keen to get into the market. In the end we found a great house and chose to be physically closer to the city rather than being further out and closer to public transport.

■ **Do you have any tips for someone saving to buy their first home?**

Very early on, perhaps 12 months before we were in a position to buy, we sat down together and decided where we wanted to live. We took into consideration what we could afford, where we wanted to live, proximity to family etc. We also talked to a mortgage broker to get an understanding of our borrowing limits and the level of loan repayments that we would be committed to.

We narrowed it down to five suburbs and spent a solid 8-10 months watching the house listings in these suburbs. Every Monday we would sit down together and look at the weekends' sold properties, filtered to our price range. This gave us a very good idea of what we could afford and expect. When we came to actually buying a house, we were confident in our decisions and knew that the price was fair because we had been watching the market for so long.

■ **How does it feel to be a homeowner?**

It feels great to know we are settling in one place for an extended time, and can put time and effort into building a home we want to live in.

■ **What's the one piece of financial knowledge that you wished you had earlier?**

[Jack says he wished he had started budgeting at an earlier age as now that they have a budget, it has reduced their anxiety around spending.]

Often when spending money on hobbies or luxuries there was a sense of guilt about spending the money, but by budgeting for that, we knew that we had 'earned' the money and met all of our other needs, so could spend the money guilt free.

■ *What's your definition of financial freedom?*

Tough question and this one took quite a bit of pondering. I concluded that I define financial freedom by its antonym, financial imprisonment. Financial freedom is NOT feeling imprisoned or trapped by my financial situation and not feeling pressured to have more money.

UNIVERSITY LIFE - BROOKE

■ *What did you do for work when you were at university?*

In my first year of university, I worked part-time at McDonalds. I then obtained a job relevant to the field I was studying (psychology). I worked part-time as a Youth Support Worker in Residential Care and with NDIS clients. I also worked casually in a children's Occupational Therapy clinic as a Therapy Assistant.

■ *Did you study full time or part time?*

I studied full time. During covid, I did one semester part-time.

■ *What were the main things you spent your money on whilst you were at university?*

During University, most of my money was spent on social activities. For example, eating out at cafes and restaurants, going out to bars with friends etc. I also spent money on retail items such as clothes and shoes.

■ *Apart from how much you earned, what is the difference between working whilst you are at Uni and working in your first job?*

My first part-time position at McDonalds was a very social job and outside of my rostered hours I did not think about work/work duties. My other part-time and casual positions during university I treated as learning and development opportunities in my chosen field. Additionally, as the hours were sporadic and balanced with completing my degree, I had much less routine and structure in my life.

Working in my first full-time position in my chosen field, my days are much more structured, and I care much more deeply about my role as I plan to remain working with my current organisation for an extended period of time.

■ *How did working whilst studying help you in later life?*

Working whilst studying taught me time management. It was difficult to manage completing my degree, working to develop my career, and working enough hours to fund my social activities and lifestyle. However, it taught me how to prioritise competing demands and it taught me work ethic.

- **Are you a spender or saver? Explain why you categorise yourself like that!**

In university I was a spender! Whilst I was able to save at times for things like my first car, I spent most of the money I earned. At that time, I didn't have many savings goals or ambitions. As I have become older, I am much more of a saver. I think this is because I have more financial goals that I am working towards, and it is easier to save when you are earning more money. Whilst I do "splurge" every now and then, the majority of money goes into my savings.

- **What's your definition of financial freedom?**

I define financial freedom as the ability to live "comfortably". To be financially free means you are able to pay your bills without feeling stressed about your income or ability to save excess money to put towards your goals.

- **What's the one piece of financial knowledge that you wished you had earlier?**

I wish I had learnt "the bucket system" earlier. When I got my first job, my dad (who is an accountant) taught me to create multiple savings accounts (or "buckets") for various saving goals. Each fortnight when I get paid, I split my pay into each "bucket". It has taught me how to budget effectively and to be financially responsible with my money.

PUTTING IT ALL TOGETHER:

Your Financial Universe Checklist

The checklist on the following pages are designed for you to work out which parts of Your Financial Universe that you need to look at. This is best used in tandem with the Goals Map where you can map out your key goals, both big and small. Access this at the Your Financial Universe website www. yourfinancialuniverse.com.au.

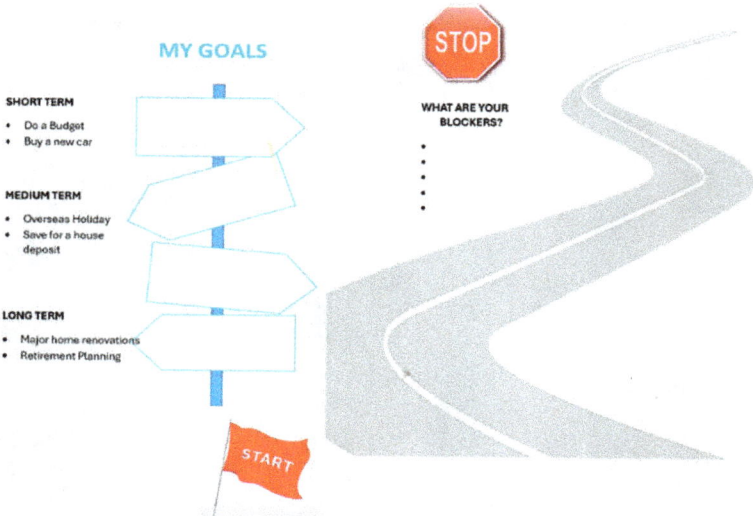

MY GOALS

SHORT TERM
- Do a Budget
- Buy a new car

MEDIUM TERM
- Overseas Holiday
- Save for a house deposit

LONG TERM
- Major home renovations
- Retirement Planning

STOP

WHAT ARE YOUR BLOCKERS?
-
-
-
-
-

START

MY FINANCIAL UNIVERSE	
SAVING	
$ Use the Goals Map to record your goals and where you want to go! Define a purpose for your saving. Writing things down also helps to keeps us accountable. $ Find a way of tracking your spending that suits you and understand where your money goes. $ Where are you going to put your savings? Identify the best way for you to put money aside and grow your savings, ideally somewhere that is harder for you to access.	
INVESTMENT	
$ Identify your surplus funds that you would like to invest now. Start with a small investment so that you can learn how it works. $ Set a time frame for your investment. The longer the term in general, the more risk you can take, as you have a longer time to ride out the bumps in the market. Remember the power of compounding! $ Find an investment platform that is right for you, that meets your investment strategy and is easy to use. There are many out there, so do some research to learn what might work for you. Using a comparison site such as Canstar can be a good start. https://www.canstar.com.au/online-trading/best-share-trading-platforms/ $ Keep learning and educating yourself about the market and your investment so that you can make informed choices, particularly when buying and/or selling.	

SUPERANNUATION

$ Check who your superannuation provider is. You can do this through your employer or your ATO account.

$ Set up member online access so that you can use the different tools and forms available, as well as make changes to your account.

$ Review your asset allocation for your investments in-cluding superannuation. Prepare a pie chart if you can and consider whether it meets your needs. Are you comfortable with your investment mix?

$ What other investment options are there? Would they better suit you and how can you make changes? Most superannuation providers have these details on their website.

$ Check your current death beneficiary nomination.

INSURANCE

$ Do you need insurance? Think about the following questions:

    $ If my home or contents were lost in a fire, do I have the funds to rebuild/replace?

    $ If my car was stolen, what would be the implica-tions? Would I need to replace the car for work purposes, for example? Could I afford to do so?

    $ What would happen if I was not able to work for a period of time? Would I be able to pay my debt, fund my lifestyle, look after my family?

$ Insurance can be expensive. **Comparison web-sites** can help you find something that is afford-able and meets your needs.

ESTATE PLANNING

$ Do you have a will in place? Who would receive your assets if something happened?

$ Who would manage your affairs if something happened to you? Although we don't want to think about this, consider a power of attorney that allows someone else to act on your behalf, like a parent or sibling, when you are unable to act for yourself.

ACKNOWLEDGEMENTS

This book came about because of the number of young people I came across in my teaching and career who didn't receive the basic information and financial education they needed for the real world. Getting a good financial start can have such an impact later in life.

My nieces and nephews were so supportive of the idea of this book, they kept me motivated to keep writing and get the message out there. Thanks also to those who contributed their own stories: Jack and Sophie, Brooke, Alice and Angus.

To my family, Paul, Ruby, Finn and Ted, thanks for being there for me and giving me the time and space to pursue my passion for education and financial literacy. To Mum and Dad who taught me so many life lessons, financial and otherwise, and who have been unwavering supporters.

A few extra shout outs: Dr. J. Diggle, a constant support, advocate and mentor; the Movers and Shakers, sounding board for all ideas whilst keeping me active; The A Team besties (plus ones); the many education organisations that have entrusted me to do what I love and teach; the many friends who loved my idea and encouraged me to keep at it; and Hazel the super pooch who is just a bundle of love.

BIBLIOGRAPHY

Accounting Triangle, Accounting Elements, http://www.accountingtriangle.com.au/accountingelements.html, 2019, Viewed 14/06/2024

Accounting Triangle, Accounting Equation, http://www.accountingtriangle.com.au/accountingequation.html, 2019, Viewed 14/06/2024

Afterpay, How It Works, https://www.afterpay.com/en-AU/how-it-works, 2024, Viewed 10/06/2024

Australian Prudential Regulatory Authority (APRA), Financial Claims Scheme, 2024, https://www.apra.gov.au/financial-claims-scheme-0 , Viewed 10/06/2024

ASIC and Moneysmart Network, Young People and Money, December 2021 https://files.moneysmart.gov.au/media/wjmncxvz/

young-people-and-money-report.pdf

ASIC and Moneysmart Network, Young People and Money – Survey Snapshot, https://files.moneysmart.gov.au/media/kjvjabp5/young-people-and-money-survey-snapshot.pdf, December 2021

Australian Bureau of Statistics, Unemployment, https://www.abs.gov.au/statistics/detailed-methodology-information/concepts-sources-methods/labour-statistics-concepts-sources-and-methods/2021/concepts-and-sources/unemployment#:~:text=Unemployed%20people%20are%20defined%20as%20all%20those%20of,to%20take%20up%20employment%20given%20a%20job%20opportunity., 15th February, 2022, Viewed 13/09/2024

Australian Government, Higher Education Loan Program (HELP), Department of Education, https://www.education.gov.au/higher-education-funding/help, 2021, Viewed 13/07/2024

Australian Government, Loan Repayment, StudyAssist, https://www.studyassist.gov.au/paying-back-your-loan/loan-repayment, 2024, Viewed 14/07/2023

Australian Government, Total Resourcing for a Commonwealth Supported Place by Discipline – 2024, Department of Education, 2024

Australian Government, myGovID Home, https://www.mygovid.gov.au/, 2024, Viewed 25/04/2024

Australian Government, How to Set Up myGovID, https://www.mygovid.gov.au/set-up, 2024, Viewed 2/08/2024

Australian Government, Services Australia, Enrolling in Medicare, https://www.servicesaustralia.gov.au/enrolling-medicare?context=60092, 24th June 2024, Viewed 13/09/2024

Australian Prudential Regulatory Authority, www.apra.gov.au, 2024

Australian Signals Directorate, https://www.cyber.gov.au/, Australian Government, 2024, Viewed 14/06/2024

Australian Stock Exchange, www.asx.com.au

Australian Stock Exchange, Understanding Managed Funds, https://www.asx.com.au/mfund/education.htm, 2024, Viewed 26/07/2024

Australian Stock Exchange (ASX), Buying and Selling Shares and Investment Products on ASX, getting-started-in-shares-brochures-3-buying-and-selling-shares-and-investment-products-on-asx.pdf, October 2022

Australian Super, Hands-Off & Diversified Super Account – Balanced Option, https://www.australiansuper.com/investments/your-investment-options/pre-mixed-investment-choice, 2024, Viewed 17/04/2024

Australian Tax Office, GST, https://www.ato.gov.au/Business/GST/, Viewed 13/07/2024

Australian Tax Office, Australian Resident Tax Rates, https://www.ato.gov.au/tax-rates-and-codes/tax-rates-australian-residents, 2024, Viewed 24/08/2024

Australian Tax Office, How to Lodge Your Tax Return, https://www.ato.gov.au/individuals-and-families/your-tax-return/how-to-lodge-your-tax-return, 2024, Viewed 24/08/2024

Australian Tax Office, Changes to Company Tax Rates, https://www.ato.gov.au/tax-rates-and-codes/company-tax-rate-changes?page=1#Base_rate_entity_company_tax_rate, 20th June 2024, Viewed 13/09/2024

Australian Tax Office, What Is a Tax File Number, https://www.ato.gov.au/

individuals-and-families/tax-file-number/what-is-a-tax-file-number, 2024, Viewed 24/08/2024

Britannica Money, Bank – Definition, History, Types, Examples & Facts, https://www.britannica.com/money/topic/bank , 2024, Viewed 10/06/2024

Cambridge Dictionary, Asset, https://dictionary.cambridge.org/dictionary/english/asset, Cambridge University Press, Viewed 14/07/2023

Cambridge Dictionary, Leverage English Meaning, https://dictionary.cambridge.org/dictionary/english/leverage, 2024, Viewed 13/09/2024

Canstar Blue, Compare Mobile Phone Plans Australia, https://www.canstarblue.com.au/phone/, 2 August 2024, Viewed 2/8/2024

Canstar Blue, Industry vs Retail Super Funds, https://www.canstar.com.au/superannuation/industry-vs-retail/, 18 January 2024, Viewed 13/09/2024

Chen, James, Risk: What It Means in Investing, How to Measure and Manage It, Investopedia, https://www.investopedia.com/terms/r/risk.asp, 19 May 2024, Viewed 13/09/2024

Collins English Dictionary, https://www.collinsdictionary.com/dictionary/english/credit, Collins, 2024, Viewed 14/06/2024.

CreditSmart, creditsmart.org.au, www.creditmart.org.au, 2024, Viewed 14/06/2024

Dictionary.com, Mortgage Definition and Meaning, https://www.dictionary.com/browse/mortgage, 2024, Viewed 2/08/2024

Fernando, Jason, Gross Domestic Product (GDP): Formula and How to Use It, Investopedia, https://www.investopedia.com/terms/g/gdp.asp, 10th September 2024, Viewed 13/09/2024

Fernando, Jason, Time Value of Money: What It is and How it Works, Investopedia, https://www.investopedia.com/terms/t/timevalueofmoney.asp, 21 August 2024, Viewed 02/09/2024

Fernando, Jason, What Is Present Value in Finance, and How Is It Calculated?, Investopedia, https://www.investopedia.com/terms/p/presentvalue.asp, 27 June 2024, Viewed 2/08/2024

Hayes, Adam, Investment: How and Where to Invest, Investopedia, https://www.investopedia.com/terms/i/investment.asp#:~:text=An%20invest-ment%20is%20an%20asset%20or%20item%20acquired,in%20the%20value%20of%20an%20asset%20over%20time., May 31 2024, Viewed 26/07/2024

Hayes, Adam, Line of Credit (LOC) Definition, Types and Examples, Investopedia, https://www.investopedia.com/terms/l/lineofcredit.asp, April 3, 2024, Viewed 26/07/2024

Hayes, Adam, What Nasdaq Is, History and Financial Performance, Investopedia, https://www.investopedia.com/terms/n/nasdaq.asp#:~:-text=Nasdaq%20is%20an%20online%20global%20marketplace%20for%20buying,world%27s%20technology%20giants%20are%20listed%20on%20the%20Nasdaq., 20 March 2024, Viewed 13/09/2024

Hayes, Adam, Zombie Debt, Investopedia, https://www.investopedia.com/terms/z/zombie-debt.asp, July 29, 2021, Viewed 25/08/2024

Healthdirect Australia, What Is Medicare?, https://www.healthdirect.gov.au/what-is-medicare, 2024, Viewed 31/07/2024

HESTA, Spender or Saver Quiz, https://www.hesta.com.au/members/forms-resources/calculators/spender-saver-quiz/spender-saver, Viewed 13/09/2024

IBM, What Is Cybersecurity, https://www.ibm.com/topics/cybersecurity, 12 August 2024, Viewed 14/08/2023

Investing Answers Inc., Asset – Examples & Definition, https://investinganswers.com/dictionary/a/asset, 2024, Viewed 10/06/2024

Kenton, Will, Rate of Return (ROR) Meaning, Formula and Examples, Investopedia, https://www.investopedia.com/terms/r/rateofreturn.asp, July 20, 2024, Viewed 2/08/2024

LegalVision, What Are the Rights and Obligations of a Guarantor? | LegalVision, 17 November 2020, Viewed 24/08/2024

Market Index, History of the ASX, https://www.marketindex.com.au/history, Viewed 10/06/2024

Moneysmart, Australian Government Guarantee on Deposits, https://moneysmart.gov.au/glossary/australian-government-guarantee-on-deposits, ASIC, 2024, Viewed 10/06/2024

Moneysmart, Borrowing to Invest, https://moneysmart.gov.au/how-to-invest/borrowing-to-invest, ASIC 2024, Viewed 13/09/2024

Moneysmart, Budget Planner, https://moneysmart.gov.au/budgeting/budget-planner, ASIC, 2024, Viewed 10/06/2024

Moneysmart, Investor Toolkit, https://moneysmart.gov.au/how-to-invest/investor-toolkit, ASIC, 2024, Viewed 14/06/2024

Moneysmart, Offset Account, https://moneysmart.gov.au/glossary/offset-account, 2024, Viewed 2/08/2024

Moneysmart, Redraw Facility, https://moneysmart.gov.au/glossary/redraw-facility, 2024, Viewed 2/08/2024

Morgans Financial Limited, All Ordinaries Market Chart, Viewed 23/03/2024

Morningstar, Investing Basics: How to Buy Shares on the ASX, https://www.morningstar.com.au/insights/personal-finance/169010/investing-basics-how-to-buy-shares-on-the-asx, 20 July, 2018, Viewed 10/06/2024

Morningstar, Top Performing Asset Classes for 2019/20, https://www.morningstar.com.au/insights/markets/203879/top-performing-asset-classes-for-201920, 2020, Viewed 17/04/2024

Oxford Learner's Dictionary, Risk Definition, https://www.oxfordlearnersdictionaries.com/definition/english/risk_1, Oxford University Press, 2024, Viewed 6/08/2024

Patel, Akhil, The Secret Wealth Advantage, Harriman House, 2023

Parliamentary Education Office, Australian Constitution, https://peo.gov.au/understand-our-parliament/how-parliament-works/the-australian-constitution/australian-constitution, 10 May 2024, Viewed 13/07/2024

Parliament of Australia, Info Sheet 20 The Australian System of Parliament, https://www.aph.gov.au/About_Parliament/House_of_Representatives/Powers_practice_and_procedure/00_-_Infosheets/Infosheet_20_-_The_Australian_system_of_government, Viewed 13/07/2024

Quotlr, Tony Robbins, Life-Changing Quotes to Unleash your Potential, https://quotlr.com/author/tony-robbins, April 2024, Viewed 13/07/2024

RateInflation, Australia Historical Inflation Rates – 1948 to 2024, https://www.rateinflation.com/inflation-rate/australia-historical-inflation-rate/, 31 July 2024, Viewed 13/09/2024

Reserve Bank of Australia, Economic Growth, https://www.rba.gov.au/

education/resources/explainers/economic-growth.html, 2024, Viewed 13/07/2024

Richardson, Tom, More Rate Rises Expected after July Pause, https://www.afr.com/markets/debt-markets/more-rate-rises-expected-despite-july-pause-20230704-p5dll8, Australian Financial Review, 4 July 2023, Viewed 13/09/2024

ScamWatch, National Anti-scam Centre, https://www.scamwatch.gov.au/, Australian Government, 2024, Viewed 14/06/2024

Services Australia, Centrelink, Australian Government, 16 November 2023, https://www.servicesaustralia.gov.au/centrelink?context=1, Viewed 10/06/2024

Services Australia, About myGov – Accessing Our Services, https://www.servicesaustralia.gov.au/about-mygov?context=64107, 2024, Viewed 25/04/2024

The Au Finance.Com, 10 Largest Banks in Australia, https://theaufinance.com/top-banks-in-australia#:~:text=It%20is%20dominated%20by%20four%20large%20retail%20banks,hold%20a%20combined%20market%20share%20of%20over%2080%25, Viewed 10/06/2024

The Au Finance.Com, List of Credit Unions in Australia, https://theaufinance.com/credit-unions, 2024, Viewed 14/06/2024

The Money Sandwich, Money Personality Quiz, https://themoneysandwich.com/money-personality-quiz/, Viewed 13/09/2024

Tuovila, Alicia, What Is Depreciation and How Is It Calculated?, Investopedia, https://www.investopedia.com/terms/d/depreciation.asp, May 27, 2024, Viewed 15/06/2023

Wall Street Mojo, Compounding – Definition, Formula, Calculation, https://www.wallstreetmojo.com/compounding/, 2024, Viewed 14/06/2024

Willed, Dave Kaplan, Joint Tenancy vs Tenancy in Common: Property Ownership in Australia, https://www.willed.com.au/guides/joint-tenancy-tenancy-in-common/, 2024, Viewed 26/07/2024

Young, Gina, Risk Profile: Definition, Importance for Individuals and Companies, Investopedia, https://www.investopedia.com/terms/r/risk-profile.asp, 17 April 2024, Viewed 6/08/2024

ABOUT THE AUTHOR

I have been in the financial services industry for over 25 years in many different roles, including financial advice, learning and development and education. Over my time I have experienced many different faces of financial literacy and the impact that knowledge can have on people's lives. I have seen the focus on education and compliance for advisers grow, but the general financial literacy levels in our community remain stagnant, particularly with women and young adults.

Education has been both my passion and the cornerstone of my career in many different ways. Sound financial advice is empowering the client to understand your advice and why it assists them. Educating young people is helping them to understand the economic and financial landscape in which they are undertaking their financial journey.

My experiences have highlighted the various levels of financial literacy in the community and the impact that education can have. And education should start as young as possible so that positive financial habits can be formed early. Having three children of my own, I can see that unfolding in my own backyard.

And so this book is my contribution to teenagers and young adults, to improve their understanding of all things financial. Knowledge is power and I hope that sharing my knowledge will empower more people to make better financial decisions.